PARABLES

COMMON KINGDOM SENSE

PARABLES
COMMON KINGDOM SENSE

BRIAN WILLIAMS

Parables: Common Kingdom Sense
© 2024 by Brian Williams

Scriptures taken from the Holy Bible, New International Version®, NIV®. Copyright © 1973, 1978, 1984, 2011 by Biblica, Inc.™ Used by permission of Zondervan. All rights reserved worldwide. www.zondervan.com The "NIV" and "New International Version" are trademarks registered in the United States Patent and Trademark Office by Biblica, Inc.™

[Scripture quotations are from] New Revised Standard Version Bible, copyright © 1989 National Council of the Churches of Christ in the United States of America. Used by permission. All rights reserved worldwide.

Cover Art by Megan Crespo

Published in the United States

ISBN 979-8-218-52664-1

Dedicated to followers of Jesus
And communities of faith
Whose journeys are filled with parables
Of the Kingdom of God

Table of Contents

Introduction……………………………………….… 1
Chapter 1: Farmer's Market……………………….. 9
Chapter 2: Unwanted Neighbor………………….…..24
Chapter 3: Barns and Nobles……………………….. 37
Chapter 4: The Naked Tree………………………….. 50
Chapter 5: Seating Charts……………………….. 62
Chapter 6: Prodigal Sons………………………… 74
Chapter 7: Totally Shrewd……………………….. 88
Chapter 8: Ceiling Prayers…………………………..101
Chapter 9: Meanwhile…………………………….113
Conclusion……………………………………….125

Introduction

In C. S. Lewis' classic, *The Lion, the Witch, and the Wardrobe*, Lucy was the very first human to ever step foot into the land of Narnia. Her journey to Narnia began in 1940 as the skies over London were becoming filled with German warplanes engaged in a strategic aerial terror known as the Blitz. The raids on London during World War II not only attacked such places as military targets and transportation routes, they also targeted portions of the civilian population.

The Pevensie children – Peter, Susan, Edmund and Lucy – were relocated to an old, large house in the countryside on the outskirts of London to live in the home of Professor Kirke. The large English home opened an entire new world of exploration for the Pevensie children. One day as she was exploring the spacious rooms of the house, Lucy – the youngest of the Pevensie siblings – wandered into a wardrobe in one of the rooms. When she entered the wardrobe, she discovered the magical, mythical, mystical land of Narnia.

Shortly after her entrance into this whole new world, Lucy met a faun, Mr. Tumnus, who befriended her. The original intention of Mr. Tumnus was to feign a friendship with Lucy and report her to the White Witch who ruled the winter wonderland with a cruel cold heart veiled by the appearance of a welcoming and gracious queen. Changing his mind about what to do with Lucy, Mr. Tumnus escorted her back to the wardrobe where she re-entered the world of the old English house. She tried to explain as best as she could the very unbelievable story of her journey to Narnia. Although her siblings initially dismissed her account, Edmund decided to see for himself. He followed Lucy into the wardrobe but went to a place in Narnia where he encountered the White Witch and became a subject of her evil rule. Ultimately, all four of the Pevensie children made their way through the wardrobe and entered the land of Narnia where an unimaginable adventure awaited them.

The parables of Jesus function in a way that is not too far removed from the experience of the Pevensie children as they discovered the land of Narnia. The focal message of Jesus' ministry was the Kingdom of God. His very first public announcement was that the Kingdom of God was present (Mark 1:15). Jesus' presence was a direct reflection of the reality that the Kingdom had broken into human history in a new way. Jesus represented the living presence of the Kingdom among people. Through him the reign of the Kingdom of God on earth had begun.

Although the Kingdom awaits its final glorious consummation, it has in fact already arrived. Jesus is the sign that the Kingdom is present and in its own way signifies a clear and present danger to the dark world of spiritual entities as well as to the enlightened world of the religious establishment. The Kingdom was inaugurated on the earth by the first coming of Jesus and will be consummated on the earth at his second coming. These two comings – or advents – of Jesus provide the grand historical markers of what is referred to as two-advent eschatology.

We are currently living in the "in between" period of these two advents. As such, we are living in overlapping ages. The current world in which we live with all of its brokenness, disease, and heartbreak is an ongoing reality for all of us. In this sense, the current world reflects the ongoing curse of the old age. The age to come represents the time when God will have reconciled all things unto himself. There will be a new creation altogether and the sinister villains of sin, death, and hell will be fully and forever defeated. In an inaugural way, this new age was introduced by Jesus.

The inauguration of the Kingdom by Jesus' ministry had the effect of reaching into the future and bringing the Kingdom into present reality. Although the Kingdom did not come in its entirety, it did come in part. It is very much like the early dawn of a new day. Even before we see the rising sun itself in the early morning, we see the soft light that begins to dispel the darkness which had so easily flooded the night. Jesus did not bring the future Kingdom in its full force into our present reality, but he did crack open the doors and windows in towns, villages, and cities and the future began to seep through the crevices.

Jesus opened the doors and windows to the Kingdom through two primary means – his words and his deeds. The Kingdom broke forth into our historical moment through what he said and what he did. We know his Kingdom deeds through the miracles that were performed. In the context of our everyday ordinary experience, miracles appear to us to reflect the out of ordinary or the extraordinary experiences of life. In simplest terms, miracles are experiences which reveal the fuller intensity and greater reality of the Kingdom than we typically experience. Miracles show us in a moment what the entire landscape of the Kingdom looks like. We get a glimpse that in the Kingdom the lame walk, the blind see, the deaf hear, the dead are raised, the broken are made whole – in essence, everything is restored and everyone is reconciled.

Just as the miracles reflect the activity of the Kingdom, the parables reflect the Kingdom in words. The parables get us closer to Jesus than any of his other words. They confront us with the presence of the Kingdom as an immediate reality. In some of his parables, Jesus took an observation from nature and used it in such a way that we can better understand the Kingdom. A farmer sows seed on various types of soil and we see that the fate of the seed is dependent upon the type of soil upon which it was cast. The Kingdom functions in very much the same way.

In other kinds of parables, Jesus told stories which confronted the hearers with Kingdom realities. The stories themselves are fictitious, but they are very real in their capacity to reveal the presence of the Kingdom. A father has two sons. The younger son takes his inheritance and leaves the homestead. The older son stays at home and does the work required for the homestead to succeed. These kinds of parables are intended to invite us right into the story line where we see first-hand our own place in the story and the reality of our orientation toward the Kingdom. In this sense, parables have the power to reveal what the Kingdom looks like and to unmask our misaligned conceptions and misguided notions of the Kingdom.

As the original hearers of Jesus' parables discovered, parables can turn everything upside down and inside out in a moment. In the wake of a parable, an entire worldview could be shattered as if Jesus had just tossed a hand grenade into the accepted religious practices of the most highly regarded religious leaders of the day. The purpose of the shattering is not to destroy us but to destroy the kind of religious thinking and practice that in fact keeps us from experiencing the Kingdom of God as a present reality. The power of the parables is that they re-order the world in such ways that more often than not we find ourselves needing to be broken so that we can be healed.

Common Sense

On more than one occasion my family has lovingly chided me about my lack of common sense in certain matters. One of my greatest challenges has to do with issues related to technology. What appears to be common sense to so many people seems like a foreign language to me. My constant prayer is that Heaven will be a place with lots of baseball fields and steak restaurants but with no technology. I simply cannot see how any form of technology can be useful on the other side of the grave. When my wife and I switched from cable to streaming, I was lost. It still makes no sense to me that we can have a subscription to ESPN+ and still can't watch half the games that are presented as options. Better still, I have yet to figure out why the shows on Live TV are decades old!

On some days, it would not be a stretch for me to imagine the freedom of having all my electronic devices thrown out of an airplane somewhere over the Atlantic Ocean. I recognize that I am in a fairly small minority of people and that after dropping them from 40,000 feet up, I would be buying new devices before the old ones would even have a chance to settle on the ocean's floor. However, such things as playing baseball and dealing with issues related to biblical studies and theology come more naturally to me. Although I have retired from the game of softball, I still can't imagine giving up my softball glove. It goes everywhere I go. Its many years of wear bring back memories and experiences of an entire lifetime. Likewise, my worn Greek New Testament with cracked covers and soiled pages still sits front and center on my desk.

It seems that what makes no sense to some of us makes perfect sense to others of us. Both sides of our very divided nation are touting regularly that the other side has lost all common sense. Political candidates even run on campaign slogans that suggest that they are the common sense candidate and that their election will restore common sense to our nation once more. From our very different perspectives, opinions, and experiences, we are all perhaps crying out for a return to some semblance of common sense.

This book endeavors to speak to the church about common sense. The focus will be on a particular kind of common sense – a common *Kingdom* sense. Through the use of some of the classic parables of Jesus, I will offer perspectives and insights about what the Kingdom of God looks like in the context of our communities of faith. I have had the deep joy of serving in a variety of churches for over forty years. What I have observed is that the vast majority of our communities of faith seek to be communities where common sense prevails. Although I am fully aware that churches can have an odd tendency to do things that defy any resemblance to common sense, the majority of churches at least seek to embrace some measure of common sense.

I will be making a bold proposal about common sense and how it relates to communities of faith in the pages that follow. Simply put, there is a common sense relative to the Kingdom of God that is not the same as the common sense we typically embrace in our churches. The reality is that every grand system of thinking has inherent within it that which makes common sense. Depending upon the presuppositions, views, or framework from which you live your life, there are certain things that make complete common sense to you. However, these very same things may or may not be the things which make common sense given the presuppositions, views, or frameworks of the person next to you.

Good people bring what makes common sense to them to their communities of faith often to discover that their common sense wasn't someone else's common sense. There is little room to maneuver when opposing common sense views collide. Everyone sees what makes complete and total sense to them and it can be practically impossible to see why those very same things don't make complete and total sense to somebody else who is as committed to common sense as we are. Although my common sense orders the world in such a way that makes total sense to me, not everybody shares my particular brand of common sense. Since our own vision of common sense is so clear to us, it is often inconceivable how any other vision of common sense could possibly make any sense to anybody else.

The Travelogue

The select parables that will be used for this book are those found in Luke's Gospel. Some of these parables may appear in the Gospels of Matthew and Mark, but there is a particular reason for focusing on the parables in Luke. Although many Jesus stories are shared among the various Synoptic Gospels (Matthew, Mark, and Luke), each Gospel tells the story of Jesus in a way that speaks to their intended audience. Each Gospel writer carefully selected what Jesus stories would be included in their particular Gospel. The writer then decided how to best arrange those stories to best suit the purposes of that specific Gospel.

The Gospel of Luke has somewhat of a simple design that is built around the travel narrative of Jesus. The significant moment in the travel narrative revolves around the words, "when the day drew near for him (Jesus) to be taken up, he set his face toward Jerusalem (Luke 9:51 NRSV)." This particular moment in Luke's Gospel sets the direction for the entire Gospel. At this critical moment in his ministry, Jesus sets in motion his journey to Jerusalem where he will be fiercely tried and ruthlessly crucified.

The travelogue section in Luke spans Luke 9 – 19. Jesus is making his final journey to Jerusalem. One of the very creative ways that the story of Jesus' journey is told in Luke is by the use of narrative and parable. The two are intertwined throughout the travelogue like best friends. Narrative and parable alternate beautifully throughout the entire section in symphonic chorus. Luke hand-picked which parables would guide the journey to Jerusalem and with surgical precision placed them right into the narrative. The parables serve to give insight about the Kingdom of God as Jesus makes his way toward his destiny.

Experiencing Parables

Parables come with their own challenges of interpretation. Even the disciples expressed some confusion as to the meaning of parables and as to why Jesus spoke in such terms. After the very first parable in Luke, the disciples asked Jesus about the meaning of the parable. Jesus replied by saying, "The knowledge of the secrets of the kingdom of God has been given to you, but to others I speak in parables, so that, 'though seeing they may not see; though hearing, they may not understand'" (Luke 8: 10).

As with the disciples, this probably doesn't clear the air all that much when it comes to understanding parables. For the moment, we will focus on several simple things to keep in mind when reading the parables. The primary thing to keep in mind is that all parables are directly related to the Kingdom of God. This north star is invaluable for navigating parables. The Kingdom of God refers simply to the reign and rule of God. As we have already seen, the reign of God was introduced in a new way through Jesus' presence and ministry.

The overwhelming challenge with the Kingdom of God is that it does not look like any other kind of kingdom that we are familiar with. God's Kingdom is so vastly different from our experiences and presuppositions, that Jesus used parables as a means for us to see how uniquely different the Kingdom of God was from all other kingdoms. The parables crash and burn our preconceived notions about kingdoms. When the smoke clears away, we see the Kingdom of God in ways that are unlike what we could have ever imagined.

A failure to see the eternal bond between parables and the Kingdom leads to an array of ways that parables are typically misread. Here are several notable ways in which parables are misread. They are sometimes seen as riddles as if the Kingdom were a puzzle to be solved. The Kingdom, however, is not something to be solved. Others read the parables as if they were secret codes about the Kingdom that need to be deciphered. Still others read parables as a mere form of entertainment that is disconnected from the realities of everyday life. Even biblical scholars have long debated how parables are to be interpreted. Does every part of a parable refer to a particular historical reality? Are parables to be interpreted allegorically or spiritually? Can we garner ethical principles from parables? Do parables share a common focus? Can parables have multiple meanings?

It is not my purpose to resolve academic issues regarding parables. Rather, we will simply take the parables told in story form associated with Jesus' pilgrimage to Jerusalem and seek to expose ourselves to their captivating power to confront us with the Kingdom. At the end of the day, the point of the parable is to challenge us and to evoke a Kingdom response from us. Just as the wardrobe serves as a portal for the Pevensie children to enter into the land of Narnia, parables invite us into the Kingdom of God. The significance of the wardrobe at the old professor's house had little to do with the kind of wood from which it was made, the detail of its craftsmanship, the color of the stain, or the dimensions by which it was measured.

Our approach to living with common Kingdom sense is quite similar to the wardrobe. We may not have all the analytical information about wardrobes or parables. Nevertheless, we can come to them and enter the fullness of the promise that they offer. I do not know the full process of how a steak ends up on my plate when I order a sirloin at the Outback, but I do enjoy every bite. Parables are open invitations to the feast of God's Kingdom. Once we take a bite of a parable, we are apt to discover that the common sense of the Kingdom is different than anything else we have ever tasted. It may even be different than the kind of common sense that is regularly practiced in our communities of faith.

Let's take a journey together to Jerusalem and step into the parables that present themselves along the way. The world on the other side of any given parable may very well be different than the one we are so very used to.

Chapter One:
Farmer's Market

"And in the naked light I saw
Ten thousand people, maybe more
People talking without speaking
People hearing without listening
People writing songs that voices never share
No one dared
Disturb the sound of silence."

The Sound of Silence
Simon & Garfunkel

A Parable

A farmer went out to sow his seed. As he was scattering the seed, some fell along the path; it was trampled on, and the birds ate it up. Some fell on rocky ground, and when it came up, the plants withered because they had no moisture. Other seed fell among thorns, which grew up with it and choked the plants. Still other seed fell on good soil. It came up and yielded a crop, a hundred times more than was sown.

The seed is the word of God. Those along the path are the ones who hear, and then the devil comes and takes away the word from their hearts, so that they may not believe and be saved. Those on the rocky ground are the ones who receive the word with joy when they hear it, but they have no root. They believe for a while, but in the time of testing they fall away. The seed that fell among thorns stands for those who hear, but as they go on their way they are choked by life's worries, riches and pleasures, and they do not mature. But the seed on good soil stands for those with a noble and good heart, who hear the word, retain it, and by persevering produce a crop (Luke 8:5 – 15).

This parable is popularly referred to as the Parable of the Sower. It is the first parable of Jesus associated with the Travelogue section of Luke in which Jesus is making his final visit to Jerusalem (Luke 9 – 19). This is significant for several reasons. It is actually the one parable that precedes Luke's statement that Jesus "had set his face toward Jerusalem (Luke 9:51)." All of the other parables fall on the other side of this pinnacle moment in Luke's Gospel. As such, this parable sets the stage for the parables that will be coming in fairly quick succession after it.

Another significant feature about this passage is that it is the parable that Jesus used to explain why he spoke in parables. When the disciples questioned Jesus about the meaning of the parable, he responded: "The knowledge of the secrets of the kingdom of God has been given to you, but to others I speak in parables so that, 'though seeing, they may not see; though hearing, they may not understand (Luke 8: 9 – 10).'" Jesus then went on to do something that he did not do with any other parable – he explained its meaning.

Finally, the message of this particular parable is critical for the ability to hear the messages of the parables to come. Parables are often read as stand-alone stories. We will see with each of the parables, that the narratives which surround the parables are an essential part of the parable itself. This may be one of the most overlooked features of parables. We often uproot parables without realizing that the narratives in which they are embedded are important for how we read them. Extracting parables from the surrounding story line is like pulling a thread in a sweater – it usually makes things much worse.

Narrative Context

It is significant to note that the immediate context of this parable took place as Jesus was traveling from one town and village to another as he proclaimed the good news of the Kingdom of God. Luke took great care to mention that along with the disciples there were several women who had been cured of evil spirits and diseases who were part of the entourage.

Among the many women who followed Jesus, he specifically mentioned Mary Magdalene from whom seven spirits had been cast out; Joanna the wife of Chuza, who was the manager of Herod's household; and Susanna.

Luke's mention of these women, as well as the mention of many unnamed women, serves to prepare for the upcoming parable. What other explanation could possibly account for the reality that the women mentioned by name were those who heard the message of the Kingdom and whose hearts were receptive to what they heard? The casting out of the evil spirits or the healing from diseases was directly related to their hearing of the message of Jesus.

There are four stories prior to this parable which shape the narrative context. These stories appear to be totally unconnected to each other. However, there is a stream which emerges through these very separate stories that binds them together. The stream becomes a rushing river by the time we get to the parable.

In the first story, Jesus had entered Capernaum after speaking to a crowd. A centurion's servant was sick and about to die. When the centurion heard of Jesus' presence in the city he sent some elders of the Jews to ask Jesus to come and heal his son. After pleading earnestly with Jesus, Jesus went with them. As they were nearing the house of the centurion, friends of the centurion came to Jesus and asked if he would simply say the word and his servant would be healed. The centurion relayed through friends that he did not feel worthy of having Jesus in his home. Upon hearing these words from the friends of the centurion, Jesus was amazed. He turned to the crowd that had been following him and declared that he had not found such great faith even among the Israelites. When the messengers returned to the centurion's house they found that the servant was completely well.

In the second story, Jesus went into the town of Nain accompanied by his disciples and a large crowd. As Jesus neared the town gate he encountered a procession in which a widow's only son was being carried to burial. Along with the large crowd that had followed Jesus, there was also a large crowd with this grieving mother. Jesus approached the coffin, touched it, and spoke not to the mother, but rather to the corpse – "Young man, I say to you, get up!" The son immediately arose from the coffin and began to talk. All the people were filled with awe and declared that a great prophet had come and that God had come to help his people.

The third story is one in which John the Baptist sent two of his disciples to Jesus to ask if he were the one who was "expected" or if they should expect someone else. John's messengers happened to arrive at a time when Jesus was engaged heavily in his healing ministry. Jesus commissioned the disciples with these words: "Go back and report to John what you have *seen* and *heard*. The blind receive sight, the lame walk, those who have leprosy are cured, the deaf hear, the dead are raised, and the good news is preached to the poor (Luke 7:22)." After the disciples of John returned to him, Luke went on to say that "all the people, even the tax collectors, when they *heard* Jesus' words, acknowledged that God's way was right, because they had been baptized by John (Luke 7:29)." In contrast, the Pharisees and the experts in the law rejected God's purposes.

The fourth story is a moving encounter between Jesus and a woman who was a town sinner. The story took place at a Pharisee's house during dinner. Entering the house with a jar of perfume, the woman stood behind Jesus weeping. She then began to wet his feet with her tears. Wiping his feet with her hair, she then poured precious perfume on Jesus' feet. The Pharisees assumed Jesus was not a prophet since he did not know the kind of woman this was. Had Jesus only known…

The Farmer, The Seed, and the Soil

This parable paints a picture which farmers and non-farmers alike can easily imagine. Jesus offered this parable not as a means to give practical advice to farmers about best current practices of farming. He is not suggesting to them that they should buy a certain kind of seed or plant that seed at a certain time of year. He is not even telling them what kind of soil to cast their seed upon. This is not a parable about the basic essentials of farming.

The disciples did not question Jesus about techniques of farming or new technology that would be helpful to farmers. Jesus did not respond to the disciples in such a way that he was surprised or astonished that they lacked such a basic knowledge of what happens when seed is cast upon various kinds of soil. The disciples understood that in order for something to grow from the ground, there must first be a seed planted. They most certainly were well aware that the soil had a lot to do with how the seed grew.

Even though Jesus lived in a very agricultural setting, he was not seeking to teach a lesson or provide an example of effective farming. There was no astonishment among the disciples as if to suggest that they were totally blown away by the fact that the fate of the seed is directly related to the condition of the soil. None of the disciples asked for a further explanation about how to identify a path, a rock, or a thorn.

The confusion expressed by the disciples had nothing whatsoever to do with farming per se. The fog-headedness of it all was more in terms of so what? What did this story about a farmer, seed, and soil have to do with anything beyond farming? Why would Jesus even bring up a topic like this? In what way could this story possibly be relevant to the disciples and what Jesus was training them to do? Was Jesus' whole point to take fishermen, tax collectors, and political revolutionaries and turn them into farmers?

When Jesus unfurled the meaning of the parable, he said that the seed was the word of God. Those walking hard, worn paths are like those who the devil comes and takes the word that had been sown in their hearts. Those on the rocky ground are like those who receive the word with joy but have no root to sustain the word. Those among the thorns hear the word but the cares, worries, riches, and pleasures of the world choke out any life that the seed might produce. Only those with noble and good hearts hear the word and through persevering are able to produce a crop.

The Soil of the Heart

As Jesus put flesh and bone on this parable, it became quite obvious that he was not talking about farming the soil, but about farming the heart.

Hearts are very much like various soils. Some people hear the word and because their hearts are hardened the word is immediately stolen away from them before anything germinates. Some hear the word and there is evidence of initial reception, but their heart is not cultivated to support the growth and the initial evidence withers away. Others hear the word but because of the numerous other interests that are in their heart, the word is choked out.

Regardless of any of the above heart conditions, the result is ultimately the same. It makes very little difference whether someone's heart was hardened like a well-traveled path, was filled with rocks just beneath the surface, or had produced thorns above the surface. The outcome was the same in each case – there was no production of fruit. Jesus could have easily described even further scenarios where the seed was sown and there was nothing to show for it. It doesn't really matter how many soil samples of various kinds of hearts can be detailed in this parable. The simple reality is that of the ones Jesus enumerated, not a single one of them were able to produce fruit.

Not to be discouraged by the various kinds of hearts in which the seed produced no fruit, there was the receptive and fertile soil of a good heart in which the seed not only germinated but produced an abundant crop. In fact, the crop was even more than was expected. The yield produced by the seed that was sown into the good heart was quite the harvest that could only be measured in terms of a hundredfold. What mattered at the end of the day was not a detailed analysis of various heart conditions, but whether there was the production of fruit.

The focus of the parable is that there is either a crop that comes from the seed that is sown or there is not. The determining factor as to whether there is a crop does not lie with the seed but with the soil. Just as in Jesus' ministry and as in the stories told in Acts, the word of the Kingdom was spread broadly and generously throughout the regions where Jesus, apostles, and believers travelled. The very same message was received in vastly different ways. This had nothing to do with the seed itself, but with how the seed was received. In particular, it had to do with how the seed was *heard*.

Jesus made clear that the parable was about hearing by citing words from Isaiah's vision of God in the Temple. When God appeared to Isaiah and he accepted the call to be sent, God said, "Go and tell this people: be ever hearing, but never understanding, be ever seeing but never perceiving. Make the hearts of this people calloused; make their ears dull and close their eyes. Otherwise, they might see with their eyes, hear with their ears, understand with their hearts, and turn and be healed (Isaiah 6: 9 – 10)."

Jesus inserted this reference to Isaiah's call experience right between his telling of the parable and his explanation of the parable to the disciples. This is the point at which it begins to be clear that Jesus' use of parables will be aimed at the heart and that the primary indication of whether it has been received will be through the way we *hear* and *see* the message of the Kingdom of God. Those whose hearts are fertile will hear and see the Kingdom. Those whose hearts are not fertile for any reason will only be further hardened and blinded by the message of the Kingdom.

The message and present reality of the Kingdom of God simply reveals the current condition of our hearts. It is not the message of the Kingdom itself which hardens our heart. Rather, it is our *infertile* response to the challenge and invitation of the Kingdom which hardens our hearts. This is exactly the same thing that happened to Pharaoh when Moses appeared before him and the same thing that happened to those who came to hear Paul proclaim the message of the Kingdom while he was under house arrest in Rome as he was awaiting trial before Ceasar. This is the same phenomenon that Jesus experienced as he proclaimed the message of the Kingdom and the same experience that followers of Jesus have as they share Kingdom life in the world.

Hearing and Seeing

The four stories preceding the Parable of the Sower were strategically positioned because they all reveal the same thing about what it looks like to listen with our hearts. It is one thing to hear the words of Jesus or to see the acts of Jesus with our ears and eyes, but it is another thing to listen to those words or perceive the acts in our hearts. The problem is not that Jesus did not speak and act. Rather, the problem is that when we do not receive his words and deeds in our hearts, we actually don't perceive and understand them. In fact, the words and deeds of the Kingdom have a deafening and blinding effect when they are not received.

The narratives are a beautiful model of what it means to authentically hear and see the Kingdom of God. Since the centurion was one who was himself under authority and was accustomed to giving orders, he had a strong sense of the authority of Jesus to accomplish things by merely speaking the word. The receptive heart of the centurion made it possible to experience the Kingdom without even actually being in the physical presence of Jesus. It is as if the word of Jesus could freely travel over time and place. When the messengers from the centurion returned home, the boy was already well. Jesus then declared that he had not found such great faith even in Israel. Not even the Israelites could hear Jesus as this centurion could.

In the town of Nain, the words of Jesus penetrated death itself and the deceased boy responded to Jesus' command that he rise up. The young man got up from his burial coffin and was made completely whole. Death itself could not keep this young man from hearing the word of Jesus and responding from even his coffin.

The third narrative focuses on the inquiry of John the Baptist concerning Jesus. John had sent two messengers to Jesus to ask if he were the one who was to come or should they expect someone else. Jesus' response to John through the two messengers was that they simply report to John what they had seen and heard.

The woman who entered the house of the Pharisee with her alabaster perfume and wiped the feet of Jesus with her tears and hair as she poured the perfume on his feet, heard and saw Jesus in a way that even the Pharisees sitting around the table could not hear or see him. The entire encounter vividly revealed how the words and actions of Jesus found homes in some hearts and were rendered homeless in other hearts even when they were all in the very same room.

A Heart Condition

There is no shortage of sounds and sights in our world. We live in a world of constant experiences which confront our senses. It is not so much the case that we hear and see different things, but that we hear and see them differently. We can all watch the same exact baseball game, hear the same exact commentary on the game, and witness the same game results. However, there will be various reactions to the game. Some will like certain moments of the game as opposed to other moments. Some will like certain players or teams and not others. Some will like the final score of the game and others will protest the outcome. Some will not be slightly interested in the game at all and many may have managed to enjoy a nice nap throughout the entire game.

The message of the gospel and the experience of the Kingdom function very much the same way. It comes down to a basic orientation of our heart as to how we hear and see the Kingdom. The seed of the gospel will have little to no fruitfulness in a heart that is not receptive to the seed even if there is an initial promise of receptivity. If there is no productivity which follows the initial reception, there will be no fruitfulness. The condition of our heart is the key as to whether we hear and see God. The heart is the soil upon which the message of the Kingdom is cast.

If our hearts are receptive to the seed of the Kingdom, we will begin to hear the beautiful symphony of the Kingdom. The music has always played and the sounds have always been there, we just haven't heard them because our hearts were not open to the music that was already there. The same is true of our sight. Kingdom images and vision are all around us. It just takes a certain kind of heart to see them. When our hearts are not fertile places for the Kingdom to take root, we will not see the Kingdom that is already there.

Since the music and the images of the Kingdom are already present, our hearts only harden against them when we remain resistant to the message of the Kingdom. If we do not go along with the deep and powerful currents of the Kingdom all around us, it will take quite a bit of energy and strength to hold our ground. Continued resistance only makes us better at resisting. Moses saw this play out right in front of him as he went to Pharoah and demanded the release of an entire nation of Hebrews from Egyptian bondage. There was a moment when Pharoah seemed to hear and see what God was doing through Moses. However, his continued resistance only made him better at saying "No."

Journey of Discernment

This parable is ultimately a parable about discernment. Although the seed of the Kingdom is sown indiscriminately, each person's heart discerns how they will receive the message. Discernment is nothing other than the ability to weigh things out. It is fairly easy to take a measurement of our body weight or height. It is something altogether different to weigh important issues and matters that cannot be placed on a set of scales. The big basic questions of life call for discernment. We might spend an entire lifetime trying to discern some of life's issues and never reach a settled conclusion.

One of the most challenging things for us to do as human beings is to engage in the hard work of discernment. It takes time, discipline, openness, vulnerability, and awareness to become a discerning person. It also takes a fair amount of lived experience to hone the skills necessary for discernment. Discernment is developed rather than inherited. The roots of discernment go right back to the hearts who not only hear the myriad of sounds that surround us but have developed the art of listening and seeing the sounds and images of the Kingdom all around us.

The farmer in the parable acted without a great deal of discernment as to where the seed was cast. He simply threw the seed down on every kind of soil imaginable. There is no indication that he threw more seed on the good ground than he did on hardened paths, rocky soil, or places where weeds and thorns abounded. He simply cast the seed without discrimination and it fell wherever it fell. It wasn't the farmer who decided whether the seed would grow in a particular place – it was the soil that determined whether the seed would grow. All the farmer did was give the seed a chance to grow in various soil conditions. Whether the seed grew or did not grow rested entirely on the condition of the soil.

When Jesus peeled back the meaning of this parable to the disciples, it became quite clear that this was a parable about the condition of one's heart in relation to God. The seed of the message would be sown without discrimination, but the hearts of those upon whom the seed fell would see and hear the Kingdom based on the condition of their hearts. If their hearts were good, they would see and hear the Kingdom. If their hearts were hardened, stoney, or filled with other interests, they would not see and hear the Kingdom.

Seeing and hearing the Kingdom of God speaks significantly to the matters related to the institutional church. An institutionally shaped church which prescribes how its members are to think and live typically requires very little of its members in the way of seeing and hearing the Kingdom. The messy, yet beautiful, process of weighing out the issues is often taken out of the hands of the members. They are often left at the mercy of those in the hierarchy who have done the seeing and hearing for them. As the foundation of the institutional church continues to crumble, it will become more urgent than ever for the entire people of God to develop the discipline of discernment – seeing and hearing the Kingdom of God.

When Jesus explained to his disciples what it meant to hear and see the Kingdom, he was describing to them what discernment is all about. With hearts open to the Kingdom, we are able to see things in totally different ways. We are also able to hear things we have never heard before. Churches have been beating the drum of vision for a very long time. There is a temptation to think that vision is some magical solution for church growth. The reality is that vision is the capacity to see the Kingdom that is already all around us. Those who have eyes to see will certainly see. We also tend to think that hearing from God is a unique experience that happens in rare moments. However, the world is filled with the sound of his voice and those who have ears to hear will most certainly hear.

As the church moves both backward and forward in holding the tension between its past and its future, discernment will be a common Kingdom necessity. The discernment process cannot be left just to those who bear titles of leadership. As demonstrated throughout the long corridor of church history, when the only ones expected to see visions and to hear from God are the religious leaders, things tend to go sideways more often than not.

In facing the challenges ahead of us, the entire community of faith must fully and freely engage in the process of discernment. Discernment is far too important to be left entirely in the hands of religious professionals and managers of institutions. Discernment is a difficult discipline to develop and members of churches are often completely satisfied to pay their leaders to do it for them, and many leaders are more than happy to let them do it.

When discernment is not the common norm of faith communities, things will dissolve into a cesspool of personal preferences. I have spent my ministry years in the context of churches where voting on church matters mattered more than any other thing that they did. What is most troublesome about this particular form of church governance is that the vote of an undiscerning person counts as much as the vote of a discerning person. When people are not seeing and hearing the Kingdom, you can count on the fact they will be voting their personal preference.

Discernment is the means by which communities of faith can live together as family and enjoy unity. Since discernment is a process rather than a product, followers of Jesus who are faithfully engaged in the discernment process may not always be agreed on everything they hear and see, but they will be moving in the same general direction as others whose hearts are open to the seed of the message of the Kingdom.

The Seed is Cast

It is little wonder why Luke used this parable as the introductory parable to the subsequent parables and as the parable that sets up Jesus' journey to Jerusalem. The last week of Jesus' ministry was understandably intense. With each step he took, he stepped further into the shadow of a cross. It would not be long before the shadow became a wooden beam from which he would hang. As the distinct skyline of the great city of Jerusalem came into view, he could already see what was to unfold and hear the sounds of both those who stood ready to welcome him as well as those who stood ready to crucify him.

The journey of discernment can be rough and painful. The very things that churches often try to protect themselves from are sometimes the very things to which we are called. We might not want to take up a cross and follow, but those are still the terms. Yet, as we choose to follow and open our hearts to the life of the Kingdom, we are often left wondering why we would have chosen anything else. When we see the Kingdom in our very midst and hear the sounds of the Kingdom all around us, we would have it no other way.

The communities of faith which lead us into tomorrow will require us to be deeply discerning. Once the busy noise of the institutionalized church has nothing left to say, perhaps we can actually enjoy the sound of silence only to discover that we have never heard or seen anything quite like it before. The silencing of mere religion may serve as a reminder that silence is indeed golden – especially when it is filled with the sights and sounds of the Kingdom of God.

Although we cannot unhear and unsee things, we can learn to hear and see things that we have never experienced. When we do not see and hear the Kingdom, is isn't because the Kingdom is not present – it is because we simply did not have the capacity of heart to see and hear the Kingdom. When the Israelites were advancing on the Moabites, Balaam had been hired to bring a curse on the enemy. However, when the Hebrews approached the Moabites, God said that he had blessed them. As Balaam and his donkey made their way to Moab, an angel of the Lord appeared on the road. After that the angel appeared on a narrow path and then again at a place in the road where it was too narrow to turn around. In each case the donkey saw the angel of the Lord and knew to turn back, but Balaam saw nothing and could not understand why his donkey was being so obstinate. After Balaam beat his donkey three times, God opened the mouth of the donkey and the donkey asked his master why he had beaten him. The donkey also declared that his master had made a fool of him.

When our hearts are receptive to the Kingdom, we will see, hear, and speak of new things. We will also learn how to see things differently, hear new sounds, and speak fresh words. The institutional church focused on being heard. As the institution of the church is being swept away, the church must learn how to focus on seeing and hearing the world around us. For the message of the Kingdom to be sown in the hearts of the people, we can no longer expect that our neighborhoods will come to the church building to see our religious routine or to hear our message.

In order for the message to be communicated to the neighborhood and beyond, the church will need to develop the twin arts of observing and listening to what God is already doing in the neighborhood. The church does not have a great reputation for listening to the world. We will need to cultivate these particular skills. Listening to the world is a primary way that we show others the love of God. The church's inability or lack of desire to listen deeply to the world has only contributed to the blindness and deafness which is all around us.

In moving beyond institutionalism, the church must reorient its heart toward the world. We must lean in even further to listen to a holy and loving God who is the redeemer of the world as well learn how to listen to a broken and sinful world in search of redemption. Whether we are listening to God or listening to our neighbor, listening is the hardest thing to do, However, when the discipline of listening is embraced by the followers of Jesus, the Kingdom of God will make much more common sense for anyone who has eyes to see and ears to hear.

It just makes common Kingdom sense!

Step Inside

Think about getting inside a parable the same way you would get inside a concert hall or sports arena. Even before the event begins, there is an excitement and anticipation concerning what is about to happen. There is something about being in the live experience that cannot be experienced in any other way. Describe an event that you participated in as a live experience. What are some of the ways in which being in the live event made it a unique experience?

The Parable of the Sower serves a similar function as Jesus' miracle of turning the water into wine at the wedding feast at Cana. Both of them were firsts and give us our initial introduction to the world of parables and miracles. As the very first parable, Jesus offered an explanation about the nature of parable. What do hear Jesus saying in his explanation that offers insight for engaging other parables?

The things that Jesus talked about in this parable were already common sense to farmers. Any farmer would have known that sowing seed on hardened paths, rocky soil, or among thorns and thistles would not yield a crop. However, when this parable is applied to the condition of our hearts when the seed of the Kingdom is sown, what new insights emerge for you?

The purpose of parables is not that we simply understand them, but that they impact us in such a way that we experience God's Kingdom. What are some of the ways that this parable has challenged your thinking? In what fresh ways are you experiencing the Kingdom by stepping into the farmer's world?

Hearing other people is one of the most caring and loving acts that we can offer them. What are some of the things that we can do as followers of Jesus or as communities of faith that conveys to our world that we seek to listen to them? In what ways does listening to our world help them to hear and see the Kingdom of God?

Chapter 2:
Unwanted Neighbor

> "You and I must make a pact
> We must bring salvation back
> Where there is love, I'll be there
> I'll reach out my hand to you
> I'll have faith in all you do
> Just call my name and I'll be there."
>
> *I'll Be There*
> Michael Jackson

A Parable

A man was going down from Jerusalem to Jericho when he was attacked by robbers. They stripped him of his clothes, beat him and went away, leaving him half dead. A priest happened to be going down the same road, and when he saw the man, he passed by on the other side. So too, a Levite, when he came to the place and saw him, passed by on the other side. But a Samaritan, as he traveled, came where the man was; and when he saw him, he took pity on him. He went to him and bandaged his wounds, pouring on oil and wine. Then he put the man on his own donkey, brought him to an inn and took care of him. The next day he took out two denarii and gave them to the innkeeper. "Look after him," he said, "and when I return, I will reimburse you for any extra expense you may have."

"Which of these three was a neighbor to the man who fell into the hands of robbers? (Luke 10:30 – 36)."

This parable, often referred to as The Parable of the Good Samaritan, was a response from Jesus to an expert in the law who had come up with the perfect question for entrapping Jesus in a legal issue involving the interpretation of one of the most significant and well known words of the Law. The expert had found a way to possibly twist Jesus into a knot by simply asking him the question that would force Jesus to respond with the only words that he possibly could. In effect, the expert would put the answer to his question right onto the lips of Jesus himself. Jesus would simply have nowhere else to turn for a response and once Jesus had answered, he would be shattered into a million pieces of glass as the expert dropped the hammer on Jesus' response.

The expert's question was quite simple: "What must I do to inherit eternal life?" He could have easily answered his own question, but he wanted to hear it straight from the lips of Jesus. Jesus' response was equally simple. It put the question right back into the expert's court and forced him to be the one who would actually say the words lifted straight from the Torah, "Love the Lord your God with all your heart and with all your soul and with all your strength and with all your mind; and love your neighbor as yourself (Luke 10:27)."

These words of Shema represent the central affirmation of Judaism. They are the words given by Moses to a new generation of Israelites as they prepare to enter into the Land of Promise. If it had not been for a point of clarification, the encounter between Jesus and the expert could have easily ended in a state of total agreement. Knowing quite well where all of this was going to land, the expert had already baited his hook and cast it right into the heart of the Shema with the hopes of reeling in Jesus as if he were a largemouth bass.

The Narrative Context

This parable falls on the heels of a very interesting encounter that Jesus had recently experienced while in Samaria. Knowing that the time of his death was soon approaching, Jesus began moving toward Jerusalem. He would be traveling through Samaria which was a little over forty miles north of Jerusalem. The journey would take at least several days.

When Jesus came to Samaria, the Samaritans were not at all receptive to him. Perhaps they thought that Jesus was just using their roads to get to Jerusalem or perhaps the long-standing animosity between the Samaritans was still too raw. For whatever reasons, the Samaritans were not at all pleased that Jesus had come to Samaria. The reception was so cold that James and John asked Jesus if they should send fireballs from heaven to consume the Samaritans. This would be exactly what Elijah would have done if he had been there.

Undoubtedly, the idea to unleash a firestorm was born of the great power and authority that Jesus had recently given to the disciples as he sent them to cast out demons, cure diseases, heal the sick, and proclaim the message of the Kingdom. He also instructed the disciples to shake the dust off their sandals and move on from any village that did not welcome them. When the disciples returned from their road trip they reported to Jesus what they had done. For James and John, the unwelcome reception of the Samaritans looked like an opportunity to exercise even more power and authority by raining down judgment from heaven.

Prior to their arrival in Samaria, Jesus had also fed a large crowd of people with five loaves of bread and two fish. That was followed by Peter's confession that Jesus was the Messiah. Jesus then told his disciples that he would be rejected by the elders, the chief priests and the teachers of the law. He would then be killed and raised from the dead on the third day.

A little over a week after having revealed to his disciples that he would suffer and die, Jesus took Peter, James, and John up on a mountain where he was transfigured. As the disciples were drifting into sleep, Moses and Elijah appeared with Jesus and they talked about the "exodus" that Jesus would experience in Jerusalem. Who better to have an exodus conversation with than Moses and Elijah. Moses led the exodus through the Red Sea and Elijah experienced an amazing exodus as horses of fire and a chariot of fire swooped him up in a whirlwind to heaven.

After the transfiguration, Jesus told the disciples a second time that the Son of Man would be delivered into the hands of men. The disciples did not understand what Jesus had told them. An argument broke out among them as to which of them would be the greatest. John pointed out to Jesus that someone who was not among the disciples had cast out demons in Jesus' name. Jesus responded that the one casting out demons should not be stopped.

It was after this second announcement concerning his death that Jesus along with his disciples entered into Samaria. After leaving Samaria Jesus sent seventy-two others into all the towns in which he was about to go. They were given the same instructions as were the Twelve who had been sent out earlier. They returned to Jesus filled with joy at what God had done through them. Jesus also was filled with joy and praised the Father that things that had been hidden from the wise and learned had been revealed to little children – those who did not belong to religious and political power structures.

Two Peas in a Pod

This parable depicts a dramatic, graphic, and violent moment in the life of a traveler who was simply making his way down the road. Apart from being identified as a man, nothing else is said about this individual's personal identity. It was clear that the personal identity of the man who was robbed, beaten, and thrown off to the side of the road was irrelevant to the story. By contrast, the fact that the other individuals in the story included a priest, a Levite, and a Samaritan are absolutely essential to the story.

The priest and Levite in this parable are like two peas in a pod. Each of them come down the road where the man had been beaten, robbed, and tossed to the side. Both of them had exactly the same response – they passed by on the other side. Presumably, they each did so for very important religious reasons. They circumvented an obvious and present need to pursue a more pressing religious and moral need – the need to maintain their religious and ceremonial purity. As the representatives of God among the people, they maintained their allegiance to God by not engaging in this clearly God-forsaken event. For them, passing to the other side was not a way of casting their faith under the bus, it was a way of maintaining the purity of their faith.

As the day passed by, a Samaritan happened to come down the road. He was not a full blooded Jew, he was not part of the religious establishment, and he was not held in high esteem in the Jewish community. When the Samaritan traveler saw the man on the side of the road, he took pity on him and went to him. He took immediate steps to bandage the beaten man and to get him to a place of safety and rest.

The Samaritan did not consult with the religious leaders or the Jewish community on how to respond to the situation. He simply became a first responder and fully engaged the situation – even at the peril of his own life. There were certainly no assurances that another band of robbers or evil doers would not be hiding and lurking further down the road. The Samaritan not only took the life of the man who was beaten into his hands, he also took his own life into his hands.

The Lone Victim

There is no telling what thoughts may have gone through the mind of the beaten man as he lay off to the side of the road. Nothing in the story tells us anything about the man. The man who had been beaten and robbed says absolutely nothing. He doesn't say who was responsible for the beating and not even a single word of gratitude to the Samaritan falls from his lips.

We are left only to imagine the horrific scene of the brutal beating. We have all witnessed scenes like this as the events of brutal beatings are recorded and made available to us every day. We watch the horrific blows to the body and see firsthand how not only bodies are broken but how the larger family of humanity is broken and fractured as well. Given the culture of the day, it would not be surprising at all if the beaten man along the side of road would have preferred to not be helped by a Samaritan.

This is a parable not only about a Samaritan helping a helpless victim, it is just as much about a helpless victim receiving the help of a Samaritan. Perhaps as the Samaritan came down the road, the man who had been beaten prayed that the Samaritan would just go on his way. In truth, he most likely did not even consider the fact that a Samaritan would offer assistance. It would have been far more reasonable for the man along the roadside to assume that the Samaritan was there to finish the job. A previous gang had left him for dead, and this Samaritan had just come back around to make sure that he was in fact very much dead and thoroughly robbed.

The Learned Expert

It was after these events that an expert of the law stood up to ask Jesus concerning what one must do to inherit eternal life. When the expert appropriately referenced the Shema as the central statement regarding eternal life, he could not help but get one last word in. This last word represented an attempt of the expert to justify his very narrow view of who was a neighbor and his very shallow concern for the welfare of strangers. A conversation in which both Jesus and the expert embraced the same central truth now seemed to have an edge about it.

The expert of the law had thrown something of a legal dagger at Jesus and Jesus turned it right back at him in the form of a parable that cut right to the heart of his attempt to justify himself. It would have been much better for the expert to have simply recognized that he and Jesus embraced the same exact passage of Scripture as the essential summary of the Law. The expert could have simply acknowledged Jesus' answer and been on his way. However, experts are quite prone to not being able to leave something alone without having the final word.

Loving God with all of our heart, soul, strength, and mind was not an issue for the expert. He did not question a single thing about what it meant to love God. He did not even question if we should love our neighbor. The only issue that the expert of the law sought to drill down on was the scope of *who* is a neighbor. There was no push back about loving our neighbors, only a clarification of who exactly it is that we are commanded to love as neighbors. Whether the expert saw this issue in terms of a line with neighbors on one side and strangers on the other or in terms of circles with neighbors on the inside and strangers on the outside makes very little difference. Either way Jesus radically challenged the expert's notion of neighbor. The line was eradicated and the circle was expanded to be all inclusive.

The purpose of Jesus' parable was to remove all lines which separate us from the next person – no matter how near or far away they may be. The distance between people cannot even be used in the hands of an expert of the law to justify that some people are neighbors and others are not. This reimagining by Jesus as to who is a neighbor undoubtedly shook the expert's worldview to its very core. There was no place in the Law or in the world where he could possibly go and hide away from the reality that we are all neighbors. God calls us to love every person as a beloved neighbor.

The Road Less Traveled

This parable is ultimately about the roads that we choose to travel. Although this parable is popularly referred to as the Parable of the Good Samaritan, it is not at all about a particular person who was "good." In fact, the parable itself has nothing to do with being good or bad. It is not a parable that is seeking to show that the priest and Levite were bad and that the Samaritan was good. The long-standing title for this parable has thrown us off the scent of what Jesus is actually saying in this parable.

If anything, this parable could be cast in terms of the *God* Samaritan rather than the Good Samaritan. Although what the Samaritan did when he saw the man beaten up and cast off to the side of the road was indeed good, it is simply not a parable about the Samaritan being good or doing something good. Rather, it is a parable about the well-worn paths of religion and how they diverge from the path of the Kingdom of God. Jesus did not ask the expert of the law which of the three travelers who came down the road was the most religious or who was good. Instead, he asked which of the three was a neighbor to the man on the side of the road.

It is evident that the priest and Levite were occupied with religious concerns and were, in fact, following religious protocols. Under the circumstances they did exactly what they should have done in their respective roles as religious leaders. They were simply avoiding the prospects of becoming unclean by touching something that was dead. If the man who had been beaten were in fact dead, they would have to endure ceremonial purification rights to be made clean. This would undoubtedly have a profound impact on their ability to carry out their religious duties.

The Samaritan had no concerns whatsoever about issues of being ceremonially clean or unclean. In fact, from the perspective of the Jews he was already unclean. He came from a very long line of people who were unclean going back well over seven hundred years when the ancient Assyrians obliterated the ten northern tribes of Israel leaving only the impoverished and marginalized to retain occupancy of the land.

It is not inconceivable at all that a Samaritan traveling on this particular stretch of road south of Jerusalem would be considered an endangerment to other travelers. Other travelers would presumably walk around him just as the priest and Levite had done. It would have been completely unexpected for the Samaritan to offer help. Not only would it have been unexpected, it would have most definitely been unwanted.

A New Path

In moving forward, the church will need to take the path of the Samaritan. The institutional framework and mindsets that have served both as the underpinnings and overlords of the church for a very long time are rapidly vanishing. In the minds of most people who have not been part of the institutional story of the church, this has actually already taken place. Most people within the institutional church know in their minds that the institution of church is decomposing rapidly but struggle to face this reality in their hearts.

The same worn paths of religion are simply not productive for today's world. Followers of Jesus are being called to walk in different places. Places and people that were previously taboo for members of the church institution may very well be the people that we are called to connect with. The relational capacity of the institutional church is often confined to those of us who were on the inside. Very much like the priest and Levite in the parable, we have been too busy and preoccupied in maintaining and protecting the many props and propositions that hold the institution together that we are often disconnected from the world that God loves.

It is not the case that the institutional church has been doing anything bad as opposed to doing anything good – it has done a tremendous amount of good in the world. Rather, it is more the case that the institutional church has in many respects drawn lines and circles which bring us right back to the question posed by the expert in the law. By what measure do we recognize that some people are neighbors and others are not? How deeply can we draw the line or how much can we shrink the circle so that we know exactly who our neighbors are?

Flipping the Script

Admittedly, this might be a stretch for most of us, but suppose the beaten man represents the religious institution. The priests and Levites of the institution are not even aware of the coming fate of the Temple. From their perspective, the Temple will live forever and will always be the center of Judaism's most prized possession. There will always be feasts and festivals, and the city will always be filled with Jews from around the world during these celebrated times of song, celebration, sacrifice, and ceremony.

Perhaps this parable speaks to a religious institution lying on the side of the road. The religious elite can't fix the institution and as members of the institution themselves, they circumvent the deep and crippling problems associated with the institution. The one person who steps toward the battered institution is a complete outsider. The outsider has no investment in the institution and may even have been pushed aside a time or two by the institution in days gone by. For a complete outsider to be the one who attends to the institution while the very devotees of the institution walk by is quite a startling picture.

Without question the religious institution having been beaten and bruised would not at all want to receive help from the hands of the very group of people that they so meticulously have sought to keep out. This would be the worst case scenario imaginable. Perhaps the institution would have to think long and hard about its willingness to receive help from such a despised stranger. Those of us who have lived in the constraints and confines of religious institutionalism will have to attune our hearts, minds, hands, and feet to the very ones that we have been wanting to *save* or perhaps, be *saved from*.

Whether we read this parable in its most simple terms of a Samaritan being a neighbor to a Jew who has been robbed and beaten or in terms of the crippling of an entire religious institution, the same truth is left standing. Whoever is on the side of the road left for dead cannot be made whole and restored by the most capable representatives of the institution or by the institution itself. When life has beaten us down in some way and robbed us of the things that we cherish and hold, neither the institution of religion nor its representatives have the means to breathe life into us.

This parable is not a call for us to do things better than we had before. It is not an admonition for us to stop being bad and start being good. Rather, it is a call for us to order our lives around the reality that every person is our neighbor. In order for the church to press forward with the message of Jesus, it must see everyone through the radical lens of neighbor. In so doing, the world will see that our Lord is one and what it actually looks like for God's people to love the Lord our God with all of our heart, mind, soul and strength. Every time they see us loving our neighbor or loving them, they will be exposed to the love of God for all people.

In the passing world of Christendom there were very clear and established boundaries between people who were church members and those who were not. The basic worldview for many church members had to do with their view of the world through the lens of institutional church. This way of looking at the world made a great deal of sense to church-formed people. We were quite familiar with church operations, programs, and expectations. However, we were not ready for the Samaritans.

The Samaritans are not shaped by our brand of religion and church, yet they sometimes have a remarkable way of showing us what the Kingdom looks like – even when it's not intentionally what they are seeking to do. The Samaritan in the parable was not acting out of a religious playbook. However, his actions revealed what the Kingdom looks like. Whereas for some the Kingdom will continue to look like the priest and Levite, for many others the Kingdom will look like the Samaritan.

In response to the expert's answer to the question of which of the three men on the road had been a neighbor to the man who had been robbed and beaten, Jesus' final words to the expert of the law were "to go and do likewise." In the very next story Jesus and his disciples made their way to a village where Martha opened up her home to them. This great act of hospitality mirrors that of the Samaritan in the previous parable. Martha's sister, Mary, sat at the feet of Jesus listening to what he had to say.

Martha was a bit peeved by the fact that she alone displayed hospitality for the house guests while her sister simply did nothing to help with the preparations. Holding her frustration with her sister in as long as she could, she eventually went to Jesus to ask him to light a fire under her sister. Jesus' well known response to a worried and upset Martha was that all the preparations that she was making were not all that important. He even told Martha that Mary had made the better choice.

Both the parable about the Samaritan and the story of Mary and Martha are contrast stories. In a very strange way, it seems as if the story of the two sister unties everything that just took place in the parable of the Samaritan. Both the Samaritan and Martha are responding to an immediate need. The Samaritan, however, comes off as something of a Kingdom hero while Martha is somewhat chided for being overly concerned about preparations. If we had been asked which of the two sisters was a neighbor to Jesus and the disciples, we would have most likely suggested Martha. This would have been totally consistent with the parable of the Samaritan.

When the parable of the Samaritan and the story of Mary and Martha are considered together, it seems as if there might be a missing connection between them. We get a clearer vision of what it means to be a neighbor when we read these stories in light of each other. In some cases, we act like a neighbor when we respond to the beaten and bruised on the side of the road. At other times, being a neighbor means that we are sitting with listening hearts to those who speak to us.

In whatever form it takes, followers of Jesus are called to be neighbors in and to a very broken and hostile world. The high calling of being a neighbor requires both the risk of stepping off the side of the road while at the same time sitting at the feet of Jesus. What the parable and the story have in common is that in each case the institutional concerns are set aside so that the Kingdom can be more fully experienced.

It just makes common Kingdom sense!

Step Inside

The expert of the law did not come to Jesus to get an answer about eternal life. He already knew the answer to the question that he asked Jesus. His concern seems to be more along the lines of self-justification. Parables have a way of shaking us free from our justifications and explanations – even if we are experts. Consider ways in which you see yourself or the church as taking the role of the expert seeking self-justification.

We all travel down various roads, each with their own signage and boundaries. Identify some of the signs and markers that you typically see along the road of your life's journey. What markers guide you toward religion and what markers guide you toward the Kingdom of God? In what ways might you have to step off a path of religion to pursue the path of the Kingdom?

Each of our journeys have "Samaritans" along the way. These are the people that we would not typically identify as our neighbor. They are on the other side of the line or the outside of the circle. In what ways does this parable challenge you to see the lines that are drawn and to see with new eyes those who were outsiders as neighbors?

It is very difficult for us to hear the voices and receive help from those whom we do not consider to be our "neighbors." The man on the side of the road would not have expected or anticipated the help of a Samaritan. Before his brutal beating, he would have most likely resisted the very notion of being helped by a Samaritan. Consider the "Samaritans" that God has sent your way. In what ways have they shown you what the Kingdom of God is like?

Chapter 3:
Barns and Nobles

"You see I want money,
lot's and lot's of money.
I want the pie in the sky,
I want lot's and lot's of money,
so don't be asking my why.
I wanna be rich."

I Wanna Be Rich
Calloway

A Parable

The ground of a certain rich man yielded an abundant harvest. He thought to himself, "What shall I do? I have no place to store my crops." Then he said, "This is what I will do. I will tear down my barn and build bigger ones, and there I will store up my surplus grain. And I will say to myself, You have plenty of grain laid up for many years. Take life easy; eat, drink, and be merry." But God said to him, "You fool! This very night your life will be demanded from you. Then who gets what you have prepared for yourself? This is how it will be with whoever stores up things for themselves but is not rich toward God (Luke 12: 16 -21)."

The stories of rich people are often captivating. Once their stories are told we realize that the real interest we have in them is typically not in the amount of money or assets that they accumulated, but in the way they lived their lives. Rich people typically live very different lives than most other people and it's hard not to be at least intrigued by their lifestyles. What is even more compelling than what is in their bank accounts is what is in their hearts. The purchasing power, properties, and exotic vacations may be a world away from where most of us live, but our hearts are a lot more alike than we imagine.

The Parable of the Rich Man is set up by two brothers who were having a dispute over the family inheritance. It seems as if the older brother was not playing well with his younger brother. Most likely, the older brother was not sharing the portion of the inheritance that should be given to his younger brother. The situation erupted in a public scene as the younger brother demanded Jesus tell the older brother to divide the inheritance with him.

Rather than mediating the situation according to the tradition of the law and resolving the dispute, Jesus turned the entire matter away from the inheritance and toward the heart. Jesus didn't say a single word about the amount of money involved in the dispute and how it should justly be distributed according to the law. Jesus didn't say anything about fairness and justice. He didn't offer a formula for determining the amount that should be given or offer the contact information for a lawyer who specialized in these kinds of disputes.

Jesus performed a spiritually surgical move and with a handful of words exposed the greed that accompanies these kinds of disputes – as well as all kinds of greed that seeps into our hearts. He further pointed out that life does not consist of an abundance of accumulations and possessions. From there, Jesus offered the parable commonly known as The Rich Fool.

The Narrative Context

There are two very contrasting narratives on each side of this parable. Prior to the parable, Jesus had driven out a demon from a mute man. When the demon departed the crowd was amazed that the mute man could speak. Some people in the crowd shouted that Jesus was casting out demons by Beelzebul – the prince of demons. Others shouted and asked for a sign from heaven.

Jesus went on to declare that he was driving out demons by the finger of God. In so doing, the Kingdom of God had come to them. As

Jesus continued talking about these things, a woman in the crowd called out, "Blessed is the mother who gave you birth and nursed you." Jesus responded with "Blessed rather are those who hear the word of God and obey it." As all of this was taking place, the crowds were increasing.

As the crowds continued to increase, Jesus declared that this was a wicked generation. As such, the only sign that would be given to them was the sign of Jonah. In the same way that Jonah had been a sign to the Ninevites, Jesus was a sign to this generation. He further declared that the Queen of the South would even rise up in the day of judgment to condemn the current generation. She had come to hear the wisdom of Solomon, but Jesus declared himself greater than Solomon. He also declared himself greater than Jonah.

When Jesus had finished saying these things, a Pharisee invited him to eat with him. As Jesus reclined at the table, the Pharisee was surprised that Jesus had not washed his hands. Jesus then went on a harsh tirade against the Pharisees. He accused them of being like a cup that was clean on the outside but was full of greed and wickedness on the inside. Jesus declared that the way to be made clean was to be generous to the poor. He further pointed out to the Pharisees their neglect of justice and love for God. He concluded by noting how they prefer prominent seats in the synagogue and respectful greetings in the marketplace.

An expert in the law spoke up and asked Jesus why he was publicly insulting the Pharisees. This led to a series of "woes" against the Pharisees in which Jesus continued to cite hypocritical practices of the Pharisees such as burdening the people with the law, killing the prophets, and taking away the keys to knowledge. When the meal was done, Jesus went outside where he was met by teachers of the law who began to fiercely oppose him and besiege him with questions.

In the meantime, the crowds were gathering by the thousands so much so that they were trampling on each other. At first, Jesus spoke to his disciples and warned them to be on guard against the Pharisees and their hypocrisy. There would come a day in which everything would be revealed and exposed to the light. They are not to be fearful of those who can kill the body. They are far more important than sparrows and God even has the hairs on their head numbered. Those who acknowledge the Son of Man before others will be acknowledged before the angels of God. Those who acknowledge the Son of Man are not to be worry about what they are to say when they are brough before synagogues, rulers, and authorities for the Holy Spirit will give them the words to say.

After these words, a man from the crowd yelled out to Jesus to tell his brother to divide the inheritance with him. In response, Jesus told the parable of the abundant harvest of a rich man. After the parable, Jesus spoke again to his disciples about not worrying about the necessities of life – God is aware of their needs. Ravens do not have barns, yet God takes care of them. Wildflowers do not labor and spin, yet they are clothed with more splendor than even Solomon himself. Rather than worrying about their needs, they are to seek the Kingdom which the Father has been pleased to give to them. They are to sell the possessions and give to the poor. By so doing, their treasure will be in heaven where there are no thieves and corruption.

This parable sits right in between warnings and woes to religious leaders and words of encouragement to the disciples. The story of the rich man and his abundant yield of crops offers a stark visual of the difference between those whose treasure is on earth and those whose treasure is in heaven. When our treasure is on earth, we are left only to worry and the ultimate loss of both our treasures and our lives. When our treasure is in heaven, we can live with the same kind of generosity with others that God shows to us.

A Bumper Crop

This parable features the kind of bumper crop that every farmer dreams of. The farmer had done what he did every single year – he prepared his soil, decided when it would be the best time for planting, and then with high hope and great expectation planted the seed in the ground. He could only imagine that in a mere matter of months the brown soil would be covered with beautiful amber waves of grain bending in the gentle breeze.

With just the right cultivation and the right amount of rain and sun, the fruit of his labor would begin to appear.

It so happened that in this particular year the ground broke forth with the most promising yield of grain he had ever seen. Never before had he seen such a bumper crop. He had worked hard and the stars lined up perfectly for this once in a lifetime crop. The crop was so abundant that the farmer knew he would be rich beyond his wildest dreams. He could eat, drink, and be merry for the remainder of his days. He would not have to worry about the mortgage, the debts, the loans, and the monthly utility bills. With the crop in the field, he was clear of them all.

However, there was one outstanding challenge that he would have to deal with. With this bumper crop in the field, he had to figure out where to store it all. He could clearly see that the barn in which he had stored previous years harvests was not nearly large enough to store this year's harvest. If the crop could not be stored once harvested, then it would lose its value and go to waste.

In light of the pressing need to store his crops, the farmer decided to tear down the old barns and to build bigger barns. The new barns would be easily filled to the rafters and his future would be completely secure. He would be seeing a lot more of his vacation homes and a lot less of the fields. His decision to build bigger barns made lots of sense and so as the crops were silently maturing in the fields, the sounds of new construction hammered the airwaves.

A Divine Disruption

As the farmer relished in his good fortunes, God spoke to him and said, "You fool! This very night your life will be demanded of you." Once in a while there is a translation of a Greek word in the text that could change the way we typically read a verse or a story. Here is one of those moments. The Greek text uses the third person plural form of the verb "demand." The more accurate translation is "*they* will demand your life."

As it turns out this is not a parable about God taking his life away from him as popularly thought. The "they" does not refer to a Roman army that is about to raid the farm and kill the family. The "they" is not a plague that is being sent upon the community as they were upon the Egyptians long ago. The "they" refers to the abundance of grain that is growing in the fields that will soon be stored in new and bigger barns.

When this parable is heard with this slight translation correction, it goes off in a new direction altogether. The farmer is not losing his life in the sense of being killed or dying – it's much worse. The abundance of his grain is about to suck the life right out of him. The bumper crop that was going to bump him all the way up the ladder is in fact going to destroy him. It will be as if in the middle of the night all the grain in his possession put a collective hose up to his open bedroom window and sucked his soul right out of his body.

It would have been better for a sword to have been thrust through his abdomen or for him to accidently fall to his death from the balcony of his upstairs bedroom as he gleaned over his crop in the softness of the moonlight than for the grain to rise up against him and demand his life. The issue was not that he was going to die that night. Rather, the issue was that the grain would become the source of his greatest agony and his worst nightmare all rolled up into one huge universe of emptiness. He was about to be suffocated by the very grain that would soon be harvested from the fields.

Stored Up Goods

The Parable of the Rich Fool is about generosity – or more to the point, the lack of generosity. It is not a parable about farming techniques, bigger barns, or managing bank accounts. The only measure by which the farmer was rich was that he had a bumper crop and built barns sufficient in size to contain the grain that would fill them. What Jesus in effect does in this parable is apply a Kingdom value to what it means to be rich. Although the farmer had a bumper crop like nothing else he had ever seen, the value of it was not determined by the sheer amount of grain that was produced, but by what the farmer would do with the grain.

It is quite clear that the farmer in this parable was making plans only for himself as the crop came in. The crop was produced in his fields, stored in his barns, and the proceeds would go into his bank account. By any measure, he was truly rich. The purpose of the parable is not to describe the delight of one who went from rags to riches. Rather, it is to tell the story of one who managed to discover that the fuller his barns became, the emptier his life grew. The vast riches in his barns did not translate into the anticipated richness of his life.

As he gathered the grain into the barns the farmer missed the purpose of the grain altogether. Grain stored in a barn has no value until it makes its way out of the barn. Regardless the vastness of the crop or the size of the barns needed to contain the crop, as long as the grain is in the barn it serves no purpose. Unless it is used for such things as making bread, cereal, or drink, the grain is useless.

What the farmer missed out on was that the grain in his barn could have easily been used to bless his neighborhood, community, and well beyond. If the very same grain that had been used for himself was used to meet the need of the world outside of himself, the farmer would have been rich beyond imagination. Instead, barns that were filled with promise to bless were robbed by the very farmer who put the grain in the barn.

The farmer did not lose his life because something happened to the grain in the barn. He lost his life because nothing of Kingdom value happened to the grain in his barn. It sat securely on his own property and never made its way to those who could desperately use the grain to put a simple meal on their table. The farmer's interests were so self-absorbing and selfish that it seemingly never occurred to him that the real value of the grain was in the way that it could be used to bless the world.

The Discipline of Generosity

As the church faces a very different kind of future, we must intentionally develop the discipline of generosity. A very brief tour through almost any church facility would easily reveal how we love to hold on to stuff – even if the stuff does not matter to a single soul on planet earth. The simple truth is that we tell ourselves that everything we cannot let go of has value. This is how we justify storing stuff in our barns rather than blessing the world.

The best way for churches to create a culture of generosity is to embrace the reality that we are stewards – not owners – of the buildings, grounds, and bank accounts of the church. Most churches treat their property and assets as if they were the owners of them. This prevailing mindset plays right into the "us" and "them" mentality that subliminally goes with the privilege of church membership. When we stop thinking like owners and start living like stewards, we are far more likely to see ourselves in the larger context of the common human story in which we all live. Living as stewards simply means that we see our role in terms of God's Kingdom reign in the world.

Most of our church stewardship talk focuses on such issues as tithing or financial giving. In many respects this is a far cry from a biblical perspective on stewardship. Stewardship is not about how much we should give to the church or mission causes and how much we should keep for ourselves. Rather, stewardship is about the use of every resource at our disposal for Kingdom purposes. This kind of stewardship only happens when we have a clear sense of God's mission in the world and that God is even now in the process of renewing all things and restoring them unto himself.

Stewardship is living in light of this grand Kingdom reality of total renewal. Once we are engulfed with the reality of God's redemptive work in the world, then stewardship takes on a whole new life. As we participate with God in Kingdom mission, generosity flows with natural ease because we are connected to the Creator and Completer of all things. Creation is not a one and done moment confined to Genesis 1. The Genesis account is not the sum of creation, it is the beginning – the genesis – of creation.

We see the continuing work of creation in things like the recurrence of seasons throughout the years as well as the forward movement of history toward the consummation of the Kingdom. Generosity begins to get a grip on us when we realize that no matter which way we turn God is already there. No matter where we go God is already working. No matter what we have it was already God's. We get to bend our ears back to Eden's pristine beginnings and hear God's mandate to take care of his world. We then get to move forward with the promise that fulfillment and culmination are taking place in this very moment.

Generosity springs from the cultural mandate to take care of the world and to participate with God in the welfare of his creation. A mere shift in perspective literally makes a world of difference. Just as it's a lot easier to spend money that isn't ours, it's a lot easier to share things and care for people when we recognize the much larger Kingdom reality that we live in. As disciples of Jesus, growing in generosity should be a discipline that we are engaged with every day of our life. The farmer undoubtedly developed the disciplines associated with farming and producing a crop, but he had not developed the discipline of what to in the event a bumper crop should ever come.

The Mystery of Generosity

One of the most amazing things about generosity is that the math of it all never works. Obviously, there are numerical values associated with such things as our cars, homes, and jobs. These numbers, however, do not reflect the places these cars can take us, the family stories that take place in our homes, or the fulfillment that might come with a certain job. When we talk about the big issues of the meaning and joy of life on the one hand or the pain and heartbreak on the other hand, we can never manage to quantify these experiences.

We all live with the very human tendency to grasp the things that we can quantify. Holding on to them provides a measure of security and letting go of them requires a measure of risk. We generally feel safer when we are holding on – even when what we are holding on to is sinking, accumulating dust, rusting out, or withering away. Although it takes quite a bit of strength to hold on, it takes more strength to let go. This is why generosity is such a discipline.

The sheer mystery of generosity is that when we are relating to things, people, and life in terms of the Kingdom, we can experience freedom from grasping any of these things as if we own any of them. The harder we grasp, the more we actually end up squeezing and choking the very things that we so badly want.

Generosity is somewhat like Niagara Falls. Over three thousand tons of water cascade over the Niagara Falls every single second of every single day. Trying to capture the water in buckets would be futile. Yet, that is exactly what we are doing when we are not practicing generosity. When all we want to do is protect our own buckets, we are actually saying "No" to the sheer abundance that is available. This is exactly how such things as goodness, grace, and love function. If we try to store these things for ourselves and don't share them freely with others, they simply turn on themselves. When our hearts, minds, and hands are fully open so that goodness, grace, and love can flow through us, we can handle tons by the second. This is the mystery of it all – the more we give it away in acts of generosity, the more there is of it to give away.

The rich farmer had no idea that by building bigger barns to store more grain for himself, he was in fact losing his very life in the process. The God who was fully capable of delivering a bumper crop could do so year after year after year. However, there is simply no need for God to send another bumper crop when the one he did send is stored safely away in the barn. Had the farmer decided to bless the world with the crop that was always God's crop, only God knows what a different story would have been told.

Churches that have a container mentality will only see life in terms of the size of the container and the need to keep it constantly supplied. If the containers are full they can build bigger ones. If the containers are not as full as they once were or showing signs of depletion, we begin to look around to see who can be blamed or if there might be a magic bullet laying around somewhere. What container mentality type churches typically lose sight of is that although institutional Christendom comes in many forms, shapes, and styles of containers, Christianity as a movement of God's Spirit does not come in containers.

Churches that celebrate and pursue the constant moving of God's Spirit can live free of the containers that seek to capture the wind. These are churches that are porous enough for the Spirit of God to flow through them as it empowers them to live on mission in the world. It is a mystery beyond calculation that the less we seek to capture the Spirit, the more the

Spirit seems to capture us. The farmer did everything imaginable to capture as much of the grain in the field as he possibly could and stuff it in his barns. Perhaps Jesus had this in mind when he said, "For whoever wants to save their life will lose it, but whoever loses their life for me will save it."

The Generosity Gene

If there is a generosity gene, it would most certainly be shaped in the form of a cross. From all appearances the cross looks like an end game symbol. It is at the cross where death stands with outreached hands just counting off the days until we are finally and fully surrendered to it. But it is also at the cross where generosity is generated and comes to life.

The institutional church has a very long history of being the focus of the generosity of its own people. We are asked to give generously to sustain the facility, the staff, and the programs. Stewardship sermons are designed to do one thing – fill the coffers of the church. The institution forever seems to plead for our generous donations. This is why many people who were once vitally involved with their church are no longer active participants. Many churches just sound like another televangelist promising how the world will be saved and you will be blessed if you just send them some of your hard earned "seed" money. Most people are savvy enough to sniff this out the moment they hear it.

A cross-shaped generosity is an entirely different thing. It is a generosity that is embedded in the story of creation itself and a generosity that hangs on a cross. This is not the kind of generosity that simply throws money at world problems and root causes. This is the kind of generosity in which we offer ourselves to the world – or more accurately, we invite God to throw himself to the world through us. When we do this, there are simply no limits of resources. Every single thing that God has can freely flow through the cross-shaped barn of our soul.

Generosity is not an issue of lack of resources. It is an issue of whether we are willing to live cross-shaped lives. We would all love to see our world at a better place. This is not the kind of place that we can get to by passing legislation. It is the kind of place that we can only get to through the pain, sacrifice, and even death that comes through the cross. This reimagining of generosity as a cross-shaped life gives us access to God's resources and positions us beautifully to bless the world.

We don't need bigger barns. We simply need to share the grain that God has already blessed us with and not seek to store it for our own welfare. Regardless of the size of the barn, the resources that can flow through it are as high as the heavens and deep as the oceans. It all comes down to how we are postured before God and his world.

After telling the story of the Rich Fool, Jesus told his disciples that they were not to worry about their lives – what they would eat or what they would wear. Life was more important than either of these two universally human concerns. Jesus pointed out that the ravens do not sow or reap and have no storerooms or barns from which they are fed, yet God feeds and clothes them. Jesus also observed that wild flowers do not labor or spin, yet their splendor is greater than that of Solomon's. Jesus challenged his disciples to seek the Kingdom and everything else would be added to them.

It just makes common Kingdom sense!

Step Inside

We all have our own barns where we seek to stuff things that are important to us. Consider some of the barns in your own life or in the life of your church family. What are the kinds of things that have been placed in those barns? What kinds of things have happened throughout the years to the things that are in your barn?

The farmer in this parable did not lose his life because God took it away from him. He lost it because the abundant amount of grain in his barn robbed him of his life. The wheat which filled his barn was a gift from God. The farmer, however, only saw it as a way to be financially secure for the rest of his life. Consider ways that our personal or congregational attitudes reflect that of the farmer.

God's original promise to Abraham was that he would bless the world through him. The fulfillment of this promise is ongoing as God blesses the world through his people. What kinds of connections do you see between God's promise to bless the world and the discipline of God's people to live in generosity?

Generosity ultimately takes the shape of a cross. It is through the means of sacrifice that abundance becomes a reality. The math of generosity is a mystery that can only be lived out through God's generosity and blessing to us. In what ways to you or your church family experience cross-shaped generosity as you seek to bless the world?

Chapter 4:
The Naked Tree

"And what's it for
This little empty garden by the brownstone door
And in the cracks along the sidewalk nothing grows no more
Who lived here
He must have been a gardener that cared a lot
Who weeded out the tears and grew a good crop
And we are so amazed, we're crippled and we're dazed
A gardener like that one no one can replace."

Empty Garden
Elton John

A Parable

A man had a fig tree growing in his vineyard, and he went to look for fruit on it but did not find any. So, he said to the man who took care of the vineyard, "For three years now I've been coming to look for fruit on this fig tree and haven't found any. Cut it down! Why should it use up the soil?" "Sir," the man replied, "leave it alone for one more year, and I'll dig around it and fertilize it. If it bears fruit next year, fine! If not, then cut it down (Luke 13: 6 – 7)."

This parable is set in the context of a Jewish religious tragedy. It had just been reported to Jesus that Pontius Pilate had committed a heinous deed of violence against Jewish worshippers from Galilee. Although the exact cause of the incident is not recorded in Luke's account, it is clear that Pilate had designed a plot for a fatal attack upon a gathering of the worshippers. Those who relayed this horrific event to Jesus simply said that Pilate had mixed the blood of the Galileans with their sacrifices.

Presumably, the attackers sent from Pilate mixed into the crowd with the Galileans and perhaps with a signal slaughtered them and mixed their blood with that of the sacrifices they were about to offer to their God. Upon hearing the report, Jesus did not call for a proportionate attack upon Pilate and his henchmen. In fact, he said nothing at all about the attack itself or the loss of life that accompanied the attack.

Instead of responding to news of the massacre, Jesus addressed the issue that was hot and heavy on the minds of those who were present. Apparently, the concern of the crowd centered on something of a theological question – did these Galileans deserve what happened to them? The question was as old as Job himself. Certainly, these kinds of things just don't happen unless they are warranted. How could God possibly allow such a terrible event to unfold against a group of people who were engaging in an act of worship? The only possible explanation would be that they had committed some sin for which God had judged them,

Knowing exactly what they really wanted to know, Jesus asked if they thought these Galileans were worse sinners than any other Galileans because they suffered in this horrendous way. Without waiting for a response, he declared that this was not at all the case. He then told his audience that unless they repent, they too would perish. Without taking a breath, Jesus reminded them of another tragic event that took place in Jerusalem. The tower of Siloam had fallen and eighteen people lost their lives under the rubble. Jesus declared that these victims were no more guilty than anyone else living in Jerusalem. He declared again to the crowd that unless they repent, they would also perish.

The Narrative Context

In between the Parable of the Rich Fool and the Parable of the Fig Tree, there is a lengthy section in which Jesus focused on always being ready for the unexpected arrival of the master. He encouraged his disciples to be ready as servants would be as they wait for their master to return home from a wedding banquet. Not knowing when he will arrive, they should be dressed and prepared to welcome him at any moment that he returns. If they are prepared for his arrival, the master himself will invite his servants to recline at the table and will himself serve them.

Jesus went on to say that if the owner of a home had known the time in which a thief was planning to rob him, he would not have let his house be broken into. Jesus then told the disciples that they should be ever vigilant because the Son of Man would come at a time when they would not expect him. Jesus went on to explain that the household manager of the master that faithfully carries out his duties will be entrusted with all of the possessions of the master. However, if the house manager thinks to himself that the master will be delayed in his coming and mistreats those who are under his care, the master will punish the manager of the household upon his arrival.

Jesus then declared that he had come to bring fire and division – not peace. Even family members will be divided against each other. Speaking to the crowds, Jesus told them that although they could predict the coming of rain when the clouds gather in the western sky and they could predict hot weather when the winds blow from the south, they did not know how to interpret the present time. He encouraged the crowd to be reconciled with their adversaries before getting to the judge's bench lest they risk being thrown into prison and lose all of their money.

A Fig Tree Without Figs

This parable depicts the potential plight of a fig tree that produces no figs. The owner of the vineyard went to procure figs from this particular tree in the garden. This was not the first and only time he had ever come to this fig tree to find fruit. In fact, he had his eye on this fig tree for three years and for the entire duration of those years the tree had produced no fruit. In light of the fact that there was no fruit, the owner rightfully concluded that it was only reasonable to have the tree cut down and that the soil no longer be burdened by its presence.

The curator implored the owner of the vineyard to give the tree just one more year to see if it might bear any fruit. He promised that he would give special attention to this fig tree by digging around it and fertilizing it. He would bring all of his horticultural skills and apply them to this one tree. If after one year's time the tree did not produce any fruit, then it would be cut down.

The parable ends without resolution. There is not a single word about the final fate of the fig tree. There is no narrative about what the curator of the vineyard did to the fig tree to help the tree to become productive. There is no mention of the progress that was made over the course of the year. There is not even a verse anywhere to let us know if the owner of the vineyard ever visited that tree again. There is not even a footnote to let us know what the fate of the fig tree was.

A Crippled Woman

However, it cannot go unnoticed that the very next story that Luke records has to do with the healing of a crippled woman. Jesus was teaching in synagogue on the Sabbath and among the worshippers was a woman who had been crippled for eighteen years. The very mention of the number eighteen should take us right back to the fact that Jesus had just referred to the eighteen individuals who had tragically lost their lives as the tower of Siloam came crashing down upon their heads.

This particular woman's body was bent forward and she could not straighten up. When Jesus saw her, he called her forward and declared that she was set free from her infirmity. As Jesus placed his hands on her, she immediately straightened and began to praise God. The synagogue leader was indignant that all of this happened on the Sabbath. He chided Jesus for healing on the Sabbath and not on one of the other six days of the week in which it would have been perfectly lawful to perform a healing.

Jesus responded by pointing out the hypocrisy of the religious leaders. They don't think twice about untying their ox or donkey on the Sabbath and taking them to the well to give them water to drink. If they have no qualms whatsoever about feeding their animals on the Sabbath, why should there be any qualms about a woman who has borne this burdensome condition for eighteen years to not be set free? Jesus' religious opponents were humiliated, but the people were delighted with everything that Jesus was doing.

Preparing to Wait

It is apparent that there is a strong theme of preparation during times and seasons when an arrival of a certain person or event are uncertain. Servants waiting for the master to come home from the wedding banquet are to keep their lamps burning as they await his unknown hour of arrival. The wise household manager should pay the workers their appropriate wages at the appropriate time. If the master of the house has been gone for an extended amount of time, the household manager could fall prey to cheating and abusing the workers. The uncertain return of the master of the house would immediately expose the mismanagement of the manager and there would be swift judgment upon the manager.

These stories point to the tension of living between uncertainty and certainty. The servants and the household manager should be totally aware that at a certain point in time the master will come home. The only uncertainty is when that certain point in time will take place. There is both a known and an unknown at play in the stories. There are two basic options in these scenarios. The servants waiting for the master or the household manager waiting for the owner can choose *how* they will wait. They will either choose to wait as if the master and homeowner could come at any moment or choose to wait as if the return of the master and homeowner are at some future distant point and are of little consequence in the present moment.

It becomes rather apparent in these stories that Jesus' focus is on the uncertainty of the present moment rather than the certainty of the future arrival. This is not in any way to suggest that the future arrival of the master or homeowner is without significance. The significance of their arrival, however, is not so much about the arrival itself as it is about the way the servants and the household manager wait for the arrival. The master and owner will most certainly come but the issue that Jesus lingered around is how the servants and household manager had been waiting.

The significance of these two basic choices is that they impact the way life is lived every single moment. They have the powerful effect of shaping the contours of our life. Those who lived as if the return of the master or owner were immanent, lived in a constant state of preparation. Those who lived as if their return were a distant event, lived in ways that made it impossible for them to be ready for their return.

Time's a Wasting

These stories boil down to a notion that may be quite challenging for our fast moving lives. We often do not know how to live productively while we are in wait mode. All we know about waiting is how much we hate it. We hate to wait in lines, on phones, in traffic, for responses. Our basic inability to know how to wait has robbed us of a very important discipline that emerges in this parable. We have a grasp of what it means when something is worth waiting for, but we have little sense of what it means to have a worthy wait.

This is where the Parable of the Fig Tree finds its place in the story. The owner of the vineyard had waited three years for the fig tree to be productive. However, the tree failed to produce figs during that entire stretch of time. The curator of the vineyard basically made a case for waiting at least one more year. Under the circumstances, the proposition of the curator appears to be somewhat desperate.

However, the curator was able to make a case for the fig tree that rested on his commitment to cultivate the soil and give the tree every opportunity to produce. What the curator was offering was not just an extra year to wait and see what would happen, but an extra year to cultivate to see what might happen. There is a very big difference between asking for an extra year to see what might come and asking for a year to cultivate the soil. Apparently, the owner of the vineyard picked up on this difference and granted the extra year – not so much perhaps to the fig tree, but to the curator.

The stay of execution that was granted to the fig tree was granted solely at the request of the curator. There was simply no further reason for that particular fig tree to have held its ground for another day. The curator made a commitment to the owner of the vineyard to turn wasteful waiting time into productive waiting time. This would be accomplished through his efforts of cultivation. The days would still pass by – but not as idle days of waiting. Rather, they would pass as days in which the soil around the fig tree would be continuously cultivated.

Cultivating a Culture

If the fig tree in the parable were a person, anyone who has an eye for discipleship would most likely conclude that this person had not been discipled. It is certainly fair to expect that followers of Jesus would produce at least some measure of spiritual fruit. It is something of a minimal expectation for disciples of Jesus. The lack of any fruit whatsoever would certainly be indicative of a lack of relationship with Jesus.

When we take a look at the investment of life that Jesus made in the disciples, it is clear that he was engaging in the practice of cultivating life. He called specific individuals into whom he would pour his life. From among the twelve original disciples, he even called three whom he cultivated even more. While the disciples and other Jews were waiting for something dramatic and spectacular to happen, Jesus simply spent his days cultivating the soil of human life all around him.

The Parable of the Fig Tree hinges on the act of cultivation by the curator. If there had been no guarantee of cultivation, there would no longer have been a fig tree. The owner of the vineyard was more than prepared to have the tree uprooted on that very day. The tree was not saved by producing any fruit but by the promise that it would be the object of the curator's constant cultivation.

Even as this short parable comes to its conclusion, we are left with no words whatsoever of the fate of the fig tree. We only assume that the curator kept his promise and that the soil around the tree was carefully cultivated. We don't know whether the owner ever came back at the end of the year to see if any fruit had been produced. We only know that the year was not spent in an idle and wasted wait just to see what another year could do once it had passed by.

The story of the fig tree as one in which time simply marches by is one thing – but it is another thing altogether to consider that a year's worth of cultivation was provided to the tree. It is certainly not the case that Jesus has no interest in whether or not fig trees produce figs. We know first-hand that he cursed a fig tree that was all leaves and no fruit. In this particular parable, he is undoubtedly still interested in figs, but he is more interested in the cultivation that may very well give the tree the opportunity to produce figs.

Cultivating the Process

Cultivation is the long-term process needed for things to grow. Since it is a process that involves a significant amount of time, it is often more of an inconvenience than it is anything else. It requires a singular commitment on behalf of the curator who will be doing the cultivating. The kind of commitment necessary for cultivating is patient and can see the potential for fruit that may come much later. The purpose of cultivating is not to speed up a natural process, but to help assure that the process has everything that is needed to lead to full productivity.

The curator did not make any promises to the owner of the vineyard that the tree would produce fruit the following year. He only promised to cultivate the ground to maximize the process of fruit bearing. This is the same thing that Jesus did with the disciples. He spent significant time with them so that the process of bearing fruit would be enhanced. Even Jesus did not make the promise that all of the disciples would end up being spiritually healthy and fruitful. Judas heard and saw everything else that the other disciples did, but he ended up in a very different place than the others.

Cultivating is not only time consuming, it involves a high tolerance for risk taking – especially when we are cultivating people's lives. Because cultivation involves as much probing and prodding as it does tenderness and mercy, there are times and seasons in which the process of cultivation is not received or welcomed. We may all want to be made whole and live in fulness while at the same time resisting and resentful of the process that makes such things as wholeness and fulness possible.

For many years, churches have tended to think that the primary way for spiritual fruit to grow was through the development and implementation of programs. Although programs are well intentioned, they tend to bend toward the demands and needs of the institution – helping people to be committed to the church. The underlying need for people is not a commitment to an institution, but a submission to a process that enriches the reflection of God's image within us.

Owners and Cultivators

It is not difficult for us and our church communities to forget our place in the parable. Although we are called to be the curators of the garden, we are not the owners of the garden. The distinction between owner and curator goes all the way back to the original story of Adam and Eve in the Garden of Eden. In the pristine days of creation, God was clearly the one responsible for the creative activity that took place day after day. After God created man and woman he commanded two specific things. First, he commanded them to be fruitful and multiply. He then commanded them to rule over the everything that God created. They were to take care of God's creation. In this sense they were called to be curators and stewards of creation.

Although Adam and Eve were given the great responsibility of being curators and stewards of God's creation, they were not given the powers of creation itself. They could not create multiple suns, larger oceans, and more Caribbean islands. The mandate given to them was to curate, not to create. God created flowing streams of water. Adam and Eve cared for those streams of water. God created the land upon which vegetation would grow. Adam and Eve were to cultivate the land that God had created.

The Parable of the Fig Tree recalls the nature of the relationship between owner and curator. The owner of the vineyard had the full prerogative to consider the fate of the non-productive fig tree. He was free to have it uprooted at that very moment or to entrust it into the care of the curator for one more year. It was not the curator's call to decide if the fig tree should be uprooted or cultivated.

Our calling as followers of Jesus and communities of faith is that of curator and steward. The church is not something we build, it is something that Jesus builds. We are simply stewards of the gift that God has given us. It is easy to lose our footing in the garden and to think that our responsibility is that of creator rather than curator. However, it is not our responsibility to decide the fate of the fig tree. The owner of vineyard alone has that responsibility. Our responsibility as curators and stewards is to cultivate the soil around the fig tree to help maximize the possibility that the tree will produce fruit.

This is the same posture that we have as curators and stewards of God's Kingdom in the world. We do not create or establish the Kingdom – that is a responsibility that only belongs to God. However, we do participate in the Kingdom and are invited by God to be curators and stewards of his Kingdom in the world. We don't determine when the Son of Man will come back, but in the meantime we live as stewards of the Kingdom presence in the world.

The right to bring judgment upon creation rests solely in the hands of the creator or owner of the vineyard. There is always the temptation for the curators and stewards to assume that judgment rests in their hands – especially when the owner has been gone such a lengthy amount of time and it is not known when he will return. The is why so many churches have the reputation of being judgmental and harsh. The institutional church brows tend to always fashion themselves in a judgmental frown.

As curators and stewards of God's Kingdom, we have the grand opportunity to look at the world in a very different way. There will certainly be a day of judgment and reckoning, but that day and the outcome rests solely in the hands of God. The cultivating of such things as love, patience, kindness, goodness, faithfulness, honesty, and generosity are the very things which maximize the opportunity for the people that we encounter every day to grow. It may look as if there is no fruit in the tree or on the vine this year, but there is no telling what it may look like next year after we have curated and stewarded the soil around the tree.

One of the disciplines that our communities of faith most certainly need to commit to is how to be better curators of not just the planet that we share together, but the very people with whom we inhabit the earth. The process of cultivating such things as love, kindness, and joy is a lifelong endeavor. Whether we see fruit or not from these efforts, we are called to be constantly curating and cultivating. We cannot weary ourselves about when the Son of Man is coming back – he will come when he comes. Until that moment comes, we share in the calling of cultivating in his Kingdom.

It just makes common Kingdon sense!

Step Inside

There are particular times and seasons in our life in which we may feel that we are more productive than at other times. Reflect on a particular season in which you sensed greater productivity. Then reflect on a particular season in which you sensed less productivity. Seek to identify some of the things that were present during seasons of productivity or may have been absent during seasons of less productivity.

As followers of Jesus, we are all called to be curators and stewards of God's Kingdom in the world. What are some of the practices that you and your community of faith have discovered that equips and empowers you to live out the role of curator and steward?

Waiting makes up a large part of our lives. Although waiting may often feel like a waste of our time, it is in the waiting that various processes of growth take place. The issue that challenges us is not whether we will spend significant times or seasons in waiting modes, but *how* we seize a season of waiting as an opportunity to cultivate or be cultivated. Reflect on a time in which waiting provided the opportunity for cultivation to take place in your life or church.

Living productively requires us to be clear about the difference between owning things and stewarding things. Think about your own perspective and orientation of attitude about things. In what ways might we think about our possessions if we considered ourselves in terms of stewards and cultivators rather than owners?

Chapter 5:
Seating Charts

"You walked into the party
Like you were walking onto a yacht
Your hat strategically dipped below one eye
Your scarf it was apricot
You had one eye in the mirror
As you watched yourself gavotte
And all the girls dreamed
That they'd be your partner
They'd be your partner, and....

You're so vain
You probably think this song is about you
You're so vain
I'll bet you think this song is about you
Don't you? Don't you?"

You're So Vain
Carly Simon

A Parable

When someone invites you to a wedding feast, do not take the place of honor, for a person more distinguished than you may have been invited. If so, the host who invited both of you will come and say to you, "Give this person your seat." Then, humiliated you will have to take the least important place. But when you are invited, take the lowest place, so that when your host comes, he will say to you, "Friend, move up to a better place." Then you will be honored in the presence of all the other guests. For all those who exalt themselves will be humbled, and those who humble themselves will be exalted (Luke 14: 8 – 11).

Finding our place in the world is no easy task. We all seek to know where we fit within the larger context of a social setting. There is something healthy and wholesome about seeing ourselves as others see us. When we see ourselves through our own eyes, it can be tempting to assign ourselves with greater importance than we actually possess. Conversely, we might assign lesser importance to others around us. We all see the world from our own perspectives. We can see ourselves in pictures, drawings, and social media images, but we can never step outside of ourselves to see how we are seen by anyone else.

The reality of what we can and cannot see about ourselves makes social ordering very challenging. We may see ourselves as belonging in a certain place in society. Others may see us as belonging to a very different place in the societal order than we see ourselves. Every society has a particular way of ordering its own social hierarchy. In the social setting of Jesus, the primary way in which society was ordered was in terms of honor and shame. Certain individuals occupied places of honor while others occupied places of shame.

The Parable of the Guest at the Wedding Feast captures just such a moment in the ancient world. Jesus had been invited to the home of a prominent Pharisee for a meal. When he arrived, he took note of how various individuals chose their seats around the table. Those seated closest to the host were deemed as having more honor than those sitting further away. The event was as much about the social order as it was about the meal itself. Once the guests had chosen their place of honor around the table, Jesus rolled this parable out right before their very eyes and ears.

As each guest arrived they sized up the other guests and chose a place at the table according to their social calculations. A miscalculation could bring about long-term disaster as to how any given person was viewed in the society. If an individual chose a seat of honor, there was always the possibility that somebody more honorable would show up. If there are no seats of appropriate honor available, the host of the event could rearrange the guests so as to make room for the guest of greater honor to be placed in the seat of one who was less honored.

The very thought of a guest being displaced by the host to make room for one who was more honorable would be unspeakable. The displaced guest would be thoroughly humiliated in the presence of all the other guests as they rose from their seat and took a seat of less honor. The stigma associated with such an incident could last a complete lifetime. Jesus observed that it would have been much better if the guest had chosen for themselves a seat of less honor. In the event that there were to be any changes by the host, the one sitting in the seat of less honor would not be shamed. In fact, there could even be the possibility of being asked to sit in a seat of greater honor.

The Narrative Context

The story of the woman who had been crippled for eighteen years that followed the parable that Jesus told about the fig tree also has a clear connection to this parable. Since Jesus healed her on the Sabbath, the synagogue leader became indignant and criticized Jesus for not healing her on one of the other six days of the week. It is no accident that this meal hosted by a prominent Pharisee was also on the Sabbath. When Jesus saw the man whose body was filled with fluid, he asked those who were standing around if it were lawful to heal on the Sabbath. Their silence was their answer.

Jesus had just been through various towns and villages on his journey toward Jerusalem. In one town he was asked if only a few people would be saved. He replied with the exhortation to enter through the narrow door because many people will try but not be able to enter through the door. He explained that once the owner of the house closes the door no one else will be permitted through the door even though they claim to know the owner. However, there will be those who come from distant places from all parts of the globe who will take their seats at the feast of the Kingdom of God. Those who were last will be first, and those who were first will be last.

Some of the Pharisees then came to Jesus and implored him to leave the area because they knew that Herod was intending to kill him. Jesus told these Pharisees to return to Herod and tell him that he would continue to cast out demons and heal people for the next three days as he continued his journey to Jerusalem – where the prophets die. Jesus then lamented Jerusalem as the city that kills the prophets and stones those whom God has sent to them. Jesus had longed to gather the people of Jerusalem as a hen gathers her chicks under her wings.

The Set Up

As we have seen, the parables of Jesus do not happen in a vacuum. They are all part of a larger context. This parable took place in a well-conceived attempt by the Pharisees to entrap Jesus. The entrapment consisted of several individual traps all converging together to bring about the humiliation of Jesus. The first trap was that Jesus was invited to a meal at the home of a prominent Pharisee. Jesus was not known for having a warm relationship with the Pharisees, and the Pharisees were not known for embracing the words of Jesus. The very fact that Jesus ended up on a guest list of a prominent Pharisee is itself quite suspicious.

The Pharisees had undoubtedly noted that Jesus did not turn down invitations to meals. In fact, they had criticized him for not being discerning enough when it came to eating at homes of those who were known sinners. They knew quite well that if Jesus were to turn down an invitation from the Pharisees, the criticisms that had been leveled against him would speak for themselves. The Pharisees counted on the fact that Jesus was in no position to decline their offer. Jesus' response to the invitation would have to be carefully considered. Traps on either side of his response had been well set.

Another trap had to do with the fact that there was a man present who had a severe medical condition of dropsy – water retention throughout his entire body. It was no mere coincidence that this man was at the dinner. He was most likely as shocked as anybody in the village that he had received an invitation from the most prominent members of town to be present. The Pharisees had also noted in times past that Jesus had a strong propensity for healing people who clearly belonged to the lower classes and whose conditions were directly related to God's condemnation in their lives because of their sin. This man's particular medical condition made it impossible for him to go unnoticed. He could not hide behind the garments that draped over his swollen body.

The final trap was that the meal was to occur on the Sabbath. This long standing holy day had been observed by the Jewish community as a day of rest. The roots went all the way to the commandments that were given to Moses by God himself. However, the Pharisees had also taken note that Jesus had broken this commandment of rest on numerous occasions. He seemed to be totally dismissive of the law. All the Pharisees had to do was simply create the opportunity on this particular day for Jesus to do what he had clearly done in the past – break the law.

Seating Charts Matter

Whether we are at a wedding reception, concert, or athletic event, seating charts matter. They can be an indication of where we stand – or sit – in relation to the host or a reflection of our financial status. Either way, it comes down to how we recognize status and position in society. Although different cultures may have different ways to recognize status, it is the same basic concept in any culture.

The invitation that Jesus received to join in at dinner at a prominent Pharisee's house was not just an invitation to a meal, it was an invitation to a reveal. Status and rank would be on full display as guests sat around the table. The man with the condition of dropsy would be the foil and Jesus would be exposed in plain view of his harshest critics. Although there was no direct statement in the story as to where Jesus sat, it can be imagined with a very high degree of certainty that he practiced what he taught and sat in the place of least honor.

The Far End of the Table

For Jesus, sitting at the end of the table was by choice. For most anybody else, it would be by force. Those sitting at the end of the table felt the pressure of their social standing and presumably took their seat accordingly, or worse, they had been asked to move down as more important guests arrived and the host requested that they offer up their seats. Jesus' admonition to take the seat of least status revolutionizes the entire seating culture. For those who have experienced the Kingdom of God, there would be an awareness that the seats of lesser status signify a very different kind of honor – an honor that was given away for the sake of the other guests.

The food served at the head of the table is the same food that was served at foot of the table. The point of the dinner by the prominent Pharisee really had little to do with the menu. The host could have offered hamburgers and hotdogs and this would not have deterred his guests one bit – kosher dietary restrictions notwithstanding. They were still there for the one reason that they really came for – to put on full display the social pecking order of the religious elite.

With the stroke of a parable, Jesus reset the table altogether. In the Kingdom of God, the least sought after seat is the most preferred seat. This is the seat that the Son of Man takes. It is the seat that God takes in his own story. It is the seat that shows us the kind of love that God has for the world. It is also the seat which reveals the kind of sovereignty through which God reigns in the world – a sovereignty shaped by love rather than by raw power.

Most followers of Jesus resonate with the connection between God's love and sacrifice. Far fewer, however, have been able to conceive of sovereignty as anything other than force, power, and determination wielded by an omnipotent God for his own purposes and glory. This parable compels us to see the kind of sovereignty that God possesses as one that is relational and vulnerable. Those who would never be thought of as receiving an invitation to the great feast of God are not only compelled to come, they are seated at the table with the God of all creation.

As Jesus continued his comments at the table, he focused directly on the host and challenged him to not invite those to the feast who could in return extend an invitation for him to come to their feast. Rather, Jesus challenged the host to invite those who could never afford to host a feast and who would most certainly never be invited to one – the poor, the crippled, the lame, the blind. With this one grand chess move at the dinner table, Jesus turned the whole event from one that featured status for those who were prominent to one that featured blessing to those who were deemed cursed.

Immediately after addressing words to the host, one of those seated at the table stated how blessed it is for those who eat at the feast of the Kingdom of God. Jesus responded by telling the story of a certain man who prepared a feast and invited many guests. As the servant went out to make the announcement that the feast was ready, those who had been invited began to make excuses – buying of a new field, the addition of five new oxen, newly married. When the servant reported back to the master, the master instructed the servant to go into the streets and alleys and to bring the poor, crippled, blind, and lame. After completing his assignment, the servant reported that there was still room. The master then compelled him to go to the roads and country lanes and compel others to come to the feast.

The Open Table

In moving toward tomorrow, it is more important than ever for the church to focus on who gets to come to the table than perhaps on any other issue. It is so easy to get wrapped up in our buildings, programs, budgets, and reputation, that we lose sight of our mission, purpose, and calling. Churches tend to draw very tight circles around tables of fellowship, tables of worship, tables of leadership, and tables of ministry. We pretty much know who sits at each seat around these various kinds of tables. The tighter these seats are configured around the tables, the tighter we feel the noose of social standing around our congregational neck.

In posturing for the future, we would do well to reimagine our mental tables. This simply involves things such as who gets invited to sit at our tables, who is welcomed without being judged, who is invited to bring voice to the conversation, who gets to participate in the work of ministry. Tables are not only places where our stories are told, they are places that tell our story. A look at our church's guest list would reveal a great deal about each of our churches. Those who have a seat at the table could reveal everything we need to know about any church.

Not only is it revealing to take note of who gets to sit at the tables, we should also note how the table is set. Perhaps we have set the tables for the very kinds of people that we want to sit at our tables. Is it possible that what we set on the table determines to a fairly large degree who feels welcome to the table? Perhaps it is not only time to invite others to a seat at the table, it may be time for us to reset the table altogether.

The strategies of getting people to fill our pews, classrooms, and parking lots are no longer viable. Strategies that invite people to tables of all kinds of shapes, sizes, and places should become our new norm. These tables are filled with the possibility of Jesus showing up to eat and the Kingdom breaking forth among us. All of this is a simple way of saying that the Kingdom is not confined to our churches. Those of us who have been very oriented toward church life for a very long time can easily forget that although the church is an expression of the Kingdom, the Kingdom is much larger than the church.

Humility and Humiliation

Jesus turned a situation that was carefully designed to humiliate him into one in which humility was cast as an essential foundation of what it looks like to live in the Kingdom of God.

We have all kinds of cultural sins that we rail against, but the one that underwrites all of them is that of pride. Unless we are fundamentally transformed at the place where pride functions as the basic operating system of our existence, it does little good to try to fix other people's lives or to fix a church.

Although humility and humiliation may look like simple variants of the same word, they are worlds apart. Humiliation happens when the weight of shame becomes unbearable. Humility is what results when we stop submitting to our pride and submit our pride to the cross of Christ. The only healthy thing that can be done with pride is for it to be crucified. Pride is not something that we can simply manage or massage. Pride functions very much like cancer – it is deadly until it is dead.

What innumerable people have witnessed first-hand in the institutional church is the religious pride that accompanies modern pharisaical kinds of mindsets. When they encounter these mindsets, they are often shamed and judged for not sharing the very same kind of mindset as the religious elite. These mindsets have drawn very tight circles around very small tables and heap condemnation on all who are not part of their very religious club.

Whereas humiliation shuts us up in the darkest of all places, humility frees us to live in the light of God's presence and mission in the world. In fact, humility sets us so free that we can love our enemies or give our lives for the cause of Christ. When we are not being held hostage by our own pride, we can sit at the foot of the table with more joy than those who sit at the head of the table. We also have the freedom to accept an invitation to any table and invite anybody else to join us at our table.

In great measure, the church has set the table for its own kind. On some occasions, the tables are used to set traps of humiliation for those who may not be deemed to have a rightful place at the table. Only by living in the freedom of humility can we avoid being ensnared by such traps. Likewise, only by living in the freedom of humility can we extend genuine welcome and the love of Christ to those who may not share our particular menus.

The Humility of Love and Sovereignty of God

I am selecting these two particular elements of God's nature so that we can view them through humility. The biggest statement that can be made about God is that God is love. It is the leading theme of the entire narrative of redemption which reaches from one end of the Bible to the other. There are certainly times in which God brings forth judgment, but it is a judgment that is rooted in his eternal and infinite love for us and seeks to bring about redemption and reconciliation.

The kind of love that God has for us is not a coercive or manipulative kind of love. Rather, it is the kind of love which we see demonstrated in the life of Jesus as he submits himself to the mission of redemption. His submission takes him all the way to the point of death on a cross. This is not the lowest point of love, but the highest point. For Jesus, love was a bleeding out of himself for the sake of humanity. It was a very painful and excruciating act of pain.

As we engage the world, it will not be enough just to make an announcement that we love the world, we must bring that love into submission to the cross of Christ. It is at that point that the love of God moves from being a doctrinal statement to an incarnational reality. Doctrinal statements are undoubtedly important, but no doctrinal statement has the power to redeem. It is the fleshed out and lived reality of those statements that bring life. The statement that God is love cannot in and of itself save a single person. But the expression of God's love in the sending of his only Son can transform any person. Love lived out through humility can bring healing to the entire world.

The same kind of reality applies to God's sovereignty. There is a popular notion that the God's sovereignty is exercised and executed with the harshness of an authoritarian judge, tyrant, or ruler. The very notion of sovereignty strikes images of brute power and force. In the same way that God's love has a quality of humility about it, the same is true with the sovereignty of God. This is not an issue about God's sovereignty in terms of being all powerful and all knowing, but in terms of being humble and vulnerable.

If it must be put in terms of greatness, God's sovereignty through humility is greater than sovereignty through raw power. Once we have a vision of this kind of sovereignty of God, we can dismantle the authoritarian kinds of structures that have far too long been part of the landscape of institutional church life. We can begin to embrace the humble kind of authority that comes when our lives are shaped by Jesus and the reality of the cross.

As communities of faith engage further with our world, love expressed through humility should be the leading edge. It opens all kinds of new ventures into God's redemptive mission in the world. It reshapes such things as love and sovereignty in ways that are far more reflective of the life of Jesus and the Kingdom of God. Pride and vanity do not fit through the narrow door – no matter how hard we try to jam them through the frame. Humility and submission open up the entire Kingdom of God to us in freedom and fulness. The table that is open to all is where our Lord finds great delight and all can feast without any thought of who sits where.

It just makes common Kingdom sense!

Step Inside

Every culture is embedded with measures of social status. This social ordering is one very important way in which we live in community with the rest of humanity. Social status is also connected to our identity – the way we see ourselves, the way we see others, and the way others see us. This parable is one in which social status plays a very significant part. Consider the impact that social status has on your own life, the life of your community, or the life of your church. In what ways does social status impact or shape your life?

Finding our place at the table is an essential part of being human. We sit at a variety of tables including those involving family, work, church, friends. Being at the table gives us a sense of belonging and community. Consider the various tables that you sit at as part of your life's journey. What rites of passage are associated with those tables? Who is invited or turned away from those tables?

In this parable, Jesus disrupts the religious status of his day by accepting an invitation to dinner at the home of a prominent Pharisee on a Sabbath. The entire experience was rigged in ways to trip Jesus into breaking the law. In a very real sense, Jesus took the bait. He then used the occasion to reorder our understanding of social status markers in terms of humility. In what ways does humility reorient how you envision social status in your own life?

Churches have a long history of promoting and protecting their own status in the context of a community, region, or denomination. What are some of the ways in which this parable might challenge or even upset the ways that communities of faith think about their religious social status? What might this parable look like in our culture?

Chapter 6:
Prodigal Sons

"Wanna feel the warm breeze
Sleep under a palm tree
Feel the rush of the ocean
Get onboard a fast train
Travel on a jet plane, far away (I will)
And breakaway.

I'll spread my wings and I'll learn how to fly
I'll do what it takes til' I touch the sky
And I'll make a wish, take a chance, make a change
And breakaway."

Break Away
Kelly Clarkson

A Parable

Suppose one of you has a hundred sheep and loses one of them. Doesn't he leave the ninety-nine in the open country and go after the lost sheep until he finds it? And when he finds it, he joyfully puts it on his shoulders and goes home. Then he calls his friends and neighbors together and says, "Rejoice with me; I have found my lost sheep." I tell you that in the same way there will be more rejoicing in heaven over one sinner who repents than over the ninety-nine righteous who do not need to repent.

Or suppose a woman has ten silver coins and loses one. Doesn't she light a lamp, sweep the house and search carefully until she finds it? And when she finds it, she calls her friends and neighbors together and says,

"Rejoice with me; I have found my lost coin." In the same way, I tell you, there is rejoicing in the presence of the angels of God over one sinner who repents.

There was a man who had two sons. The younger one said to his father, "Father, give me my share of the estate." So he divided his property between them. Not long after that, the younger son got together all he had, set off for a distant country and there squandered his wealth in wild living. After he had spent everything, there was a severe famine in that whole country, and he began to be in need. So he went and hired himself out to a citizen of that country, who sent him to his fields to feed his pigs. He longed to fill his stomach with the pods that the pigs were eating, but no one gave him anything.

When he came to his senses, he said, "How many of my father's hired servants have food to spare, and here I am starving to death! I will set out and go back to my father and say to him: Father, I have sinned against heaven and against you. I am no longer worthy to be called your son; make me like one of your hired servants." So he got up and went to his father.

But while he was still a long way off, his father saw him and was filled with compassion for him; he ran to his son, threw his arms around him and kissed him. The son said to him, "Father, I have sinned against heaven and against you. I am no longer worthy to be called your son."

But the father said to his servants, "Quick! Bring the best robe and put it on him. Put a ring on his finger and sandals on his feet. Bring the fattened calf and kill it. Let's have a feast and celebrate. For this son of mine was dead and is alive again; he was lost and is found." So they began to celebrate.

Meanwhile, the older son was in the field. When he came near the house, he heard music and dancing. So he called one of the servants and asked him what was going on. "Your brother has come," he replied, "and your father has killed the fattened calf because he has him back safe and sound."

The older brother became angry and refused to go in. So his father went out and pleaded with him. But he answered his father, "Look! All these years I've been slaving for you and never disobeyed your orders. Yet you never gave me even a young goat so I could celebrate with my friends. But when this son of yours who has squandered your property with prostitutes comes home, you kill the fattened calf for him!"

"My son," the father said, "you are always with me, and everything I have is yours. But we had to celebrate and be glad, because this brother of yours was dead and is alive again; he was lost and is found (Luke 15:3 – 32).

Parables are designed to confront us with the Kingdom in ways that we never see coming. Perhaps no parable does this as well as this one. The inherent sting of this parable lies in large measure with the make-up of the particular audience. The Parable of the Prodigal is well known, but few recognize how important it is to read this parable in light of the immediate audience: one group consisted of tax collectors and sinners and the other group consisted of Pharisees and teachers of the law.

This lengthy parable itself is very straight forward. A shepherd finds a missing sheep, a woman finds a missing coin, and a son returns home to his father. There is great joy and grand celebration when each are returned to their rightful place. There is nothing complicated about this parable and the meaning lies right on the surface. It would be hard to miss the basic story line or to get wrapped around the axle of what is taking place in this parable. There are no hidden meanings or secret codes. Nevertheless, this parable ends up packing one of the most powerful punches ever thrown.

Narrative Context

At this point in the narrative very large crowds were following Jesus. Immediately before the parable of the lost sheep, coin, and son, Jesus spoke to the crowd openly about what was necessary to become a disciple. The words were strong and the terms even stronger. A person must hate their own family and even their own life in order to follow Jesus. Carrying the cross was absolutely essential – no way around it.

Jesus then used several examples of what it looks like to carry the cross. When a tower is built, the builder would be remiss if he failed to calculate the cost of the entire project before laying the first stone. A builder would be ridiculed for not having enough money to build beyond the foundation. Likewise, a king who did not calculate the larger numbers of troops of an opposing army would need to send a delegation of peace to the enemy while they were a far distance off.

The clear theme in both of these examples is that of being adequately prepared to follow through with a project or an event. Counting the cost in advance will save the builder from ridicule and the king from defeat. The parable followed directly on the heels of Jesus' injunction to count the cost. The connection between the admonition of Jesus to count the cost and the parable may not seem apparent. We are left to wonder in what ways does counting the cost of following Jesus have to do with a lost sheep, a lost coin, and a lost son?

We observed earlier that in terms of the parable, the lost sheep and the lost coin actually functioned as foils in setting up the story of the lost son. Once we see the lost sheep and the lost coin as set ups for the lost son, we can more easily see the connection between the builder counting the cost of a building, a king considering the cost of war, and a son longing for a new life. Each of them had to count the cost. It is clear that the son made a significant calculation and executed a plan. However, given the unruly lifestyle that he engaged in and the unforeseen famine that ensued, his calculations came nowhere close to funding his ventures. He ran out of money long before he ran out of riotous living.

Like a builder with an unfinished tower or a king with a defeated army, the younger son's miscalculations had cost him his life. He was as good as dead. As it turns out, however, it was this very death that brought him to his senses and set him on the road to take perhaps the biggest risk of his life – the return to his father. Would there ever be a place he could call home?

A Multi-Phased Parable

Many people make the mistake of thinking these are three parables strung together with a similar theme – something is lost then found. However, these are not three separate parables placed in sequence of intensity. This is one parable with three movements. The first two movements are designed to be delightful and harmless. A shepherd goes searching for one lost sheep and finds it. Everybody is glad to hear that the one missing sheep that had been lost is returned to the fold. There is no harm or sucker punch to any of those present in the crowd with Jesus as they share in the delight of the finding of the lost sheep.

Likewise, there is nothing but delight and joy for the woman who searches for her lost silver coin and finds it. Again, there is nothing here that communicates anything other than the fact that we can all share in the joy of her discovery. Our hearts are warmed by the story and we find no offence at all in either the story of the shepherd or the story of the woman. We are grateful that things turned out as they did for both of them.

As Jesus told the stories of the lost sheep and the lost coin, the audience leaned in to hear if the shepherd was going to ever find the sheep or if the woman would ever be able to locate the missing coin. Everyone who listened along to the parable was being roped in to hear the hoped for outcome. The parable brought delight to the tax collectors and the sinners as well as the Pharisees and the teachers of the law. It was simply a human interest type story which turned out well and could be easily told to young children as they were being tucked into bed at night.

The parable then moved into its final movement. A father had two sons. The younger son decided he wanted to chase a different future than the one he could have by staying home. He demanded that his father give him his share of the inheritance. Once he received his inheritance he made his way out into the world and set out for a distant country. Once he got there he squandered his wealth in wild living. After he had burned through all his money, a severe famine came upon the land. Having nothing left, the younger son took a job in which he worked for a citizen of the country who sent him into the fields to feed the pigs. While he was feeding the pigs, he himself was starving to death.

As he considered the fact that the hired servants back home had a surplus of food to eat, the younger son came to his senses. He decided to go back to his father and confess his sinfulness against both heaven and his father. He would further confess that he recognized that he was no longer worthy of being called his son. He also decided to ask his father if he could be made to be like one of the hired servants. Once he made all these decisions, he began the journey home.

While a far distance off, his father had compassion on him and ran to meet him. The father greeted him with hugs, kisses, a robe, a ring, and sandals. The father immediately called for a feast to be prepared. When word of all of this got to the older son working in the field and he began to hear the music and celebration, he became very angry and refused to go into the house. The father came out and pleaded with him, but the older son expressed his frustration that although he had been faithful to his father there had never been such a celebration thrown in his honor. Yet, the younger son who had squandered everything had been given the feast of a lifetime.

The Reveal

In the case of the lost sheep and the lost coin, the shepherd and the woman set out to find that which was lost. In the case of the lost son there is an interesting twist. As the audience of Jesus listened to the story unfolding, they would have perhaps run ahead of the story and thought to themselves that they could clearly see what the father would do after the son left home. Like the shepherd searching for his one sheep and the woman searching for her one silver coin, the father would undoubtedly go searching for his younger son.

Certainly, the importance of a son was greater than that of a sheep or a coin. Without question, the love of a father for his son would compel the father to spare no expense in searching for his son. However, in this parable the father gave the requested inheritance to his son and the son traveled to a distant land. The audience may have reasonably expected that based on the actions of the shepherd and the woman, the father would have gone out to find his son and not come home until the mission was complete.

There is no suggestion in the parable that the father conducted a search for his son. Did the father not care for his son as much as the shepherd cared for the one missing sheep or the woman cared for one lost coin? Yet, it is clear that the father waited expectantly at home and when he saw his son, even from a distance, ran out to welcome him home. The whole sequence of events concerning the father and the younger son would be somewhat shocking in an honor and shame culture.

The very fact that the younger son asked for the inheritance in advance was a dramatic way of declaring that the son regarded his father as dead to him. It was a huge social embarrassment to the family. The audience may have been shocked that that father conceded to the request of his son. They would have been equally shocked to hear that upon the return of the younger son that the father would even consider receiving the son back home – much less throwing an elaborate celebration for him.

The parable does not depict an unloving or uncaring father who was not concerned enough to go on a search for his son. Rather, this is a father who loved his son so much he was willing to embrace the "death" and social disgrace that accompanied such an unfortunate family event. It was not out of a lack of love that the father did not track his son down and bring him home, but out of an abundance of love that the father gave him his part of the inheritance and released him to a far off country without any assurance that he would ever see or hear from his son again.

It is clear that the younger son made some sort of calculation as he ventured into the unknown world, but it is often overlooked that the father also made some very serious and weighty calculations. By giving his son his portion of the inheritance and freely releasing him from any relationship and responsibility, the father was in fact taking the greatest risk of anyone in the parable. The father's response to his son was born of a deep love that only a parent could have for their child. There is a point at which love stretches beyond any calculation or measure. The builder of a tower and the king of an army could calculate the costs of what may lie ahead, but how does the father count the cost of releasing his son? The matter of the inheritance would be the least of the father's concerns.

However, the older son did not share the kind of love for his younger brother that his father did. The older brother was clearly agitated by the news of his brother's homecoming and the reception that he received from the father. The older brother did not share in the joy and celebration of the homecoming. The return of the younger brother revealed what was in the heart of the older brother the entire time. Although the older brother never left home and was dutiful in his responsibilities at home, it became clear that his heart was never in it. He was so disconnected from his father's heart that when his father was in the height of delight, the older son was in the depth of disgust.

Igniting the Fuse

Jesus reined in the audience of tax collectors and sinners as well as the Pharisees and teachers of the law as he told this parable. None of those represented in the audience could have foreseen where this parable was going and how it spoke directly to their respective standings in the community. Undoubtedly, everyone in the crowd knew exactly which group they were part of and how the other group felt about them. For a few brief moments as Jesus was telling the parable, all the members of the crowd shared a mutual interest in the story line.

As the parable drew to its end, it actually never concluded. Jesus left his audience hanging on the fate of the older brother. Did the older brother end up asking for his portion of the inheritance? Did he leave home as his younger brother had done? Was he ever reconciled with his younger brother? Did he hold a grudge for the rest of his life toward his father and brother? Did he ever come to experience the joy that his father experienced when he saw the younger son and ran out to welcome him?

As the parable was wrapping up, it began to occur to those to whom Jesus was speaking how dangerously close this parable was getting to them. At some point they could see that this parable had a direct connection to them. It was no longer a parable about a father and his two sons. It was a parable about the two groups of people who were standing right in the presence of Jesus. Not only were the two groups very distinguishable from each other, they also shared a common vision of who was accepted by God and who was not. Clearly, the sinners and tax collectors had no expectations of being considered righteous. On the other hand, the Pharisees and teachers of the law considered themselves to be the kind of righteous people with whom God would take great delight.

However, the parable seems to get things twisted around a bit. Everyone in the audience knew that the tax collectors and sinners seemed to have a lot of affinity with the younger son as he ventured far away from home. All the while, the Pharisees and religious leaders – much like the older son – had planted their stakes close to the father. There was no dispute whatsoever that the younger son was representative of the tax collectors and sinners while the older son was representative of the Pharisees and teachers of the law.

Although there were no surprises as to which son represented which group, there were stark revelations about the nature of the relationship between each group and the father. No one could have ever imagined that the sinners and tax collectors would end up being so openly received by the father and that such a grand celebration and feast would have ever been held in their honor. Likewise, no one could have possibly seen the Pharisees and teachers of the law as occupying any other position than that of being the righteous representatives of God on the earth.

For the tax collectors and sinners, the outcome of the parable was nothing short of good news, hope, forgiveness, feasting, and celebration. The open invitation to come home was staring them squarely in the eyes. The Pharisees and teachers of the law were in something of a different fix. It was as if all their religious pride and self-righteousness had run amuck and was coming unglued at the seams. The parable was holding a knife to their throats as if to kill the fatted calf or the sacrificial lamb. Yet, the father still desired for the older son to live on the family land with all the rights and privileges that go along with that of being the older son. The father still held the door open for his older son to actually live as a family member who would share the heart of the father and join in the celebration of the homecoming of his younger brother.

In Sync

Most members of churches long to find a deep sense of unity in their church, but many never find it. Churches try to foster a sense of unity by such things as doctrinal uniformity, mission and vision statements, meaningful worship experiences, fellowship opportunities, Bible study programs, mission engagements, and a whole host of other kinds of activities. All of these can certainly play a very important role in nurturing a sense of church unity.

Ultimately, unity has to do with the beating of our hearts. When we have a particular passion for something, it is common to say that we have a heart for that certain thing. Whatever it is that we have a heart for is perhaps the most formative shaping factor in our life. When we have a heart for something or someone we can't get it off of our minds. More than we are aware, our thoughts and actions bend strongly toward the direction of our hearts.

The parable of the prodigal son is really a parable about two prodigal sons. Both sons had the same exact issue, they just expressed them in very different ways. The younger son's heart of rebellion was expressed as open defiance and departure. The older son's heart of rebellion was expressed as inner self-absorption and antagonism. In either case, there was a major heart issue – neither of their heart's beat with the father's heart. In their own ways, they were out of sync with their father and were definitely out of sync with each other.

Only when the father released his younger son was it possible for the son to come to a place where he would eventually share his father's heart. For a very long time there has been a heartbeat for the institutional church in the western world. At times, this heartbeat pounded so loudly that the vision of any other kind of church apart from an institutional vision was not even on the radar. Only faint murmurs were heard from time to time but they were quickly dismissed as irregular heart rhythms.

The once strong heartbeat of the institutional church has now become a much weaker pulse in our midst. During this moment of time some churches will simply bleed out and others will leverage the moment to become a different kind of church – one which functions and feels like an organism rather than an organization. However, for this to become a reality, it will be necessary for the church to die a certain kind of death in order to engage a certain kind of life. The basic difference between the two sons in the parable was that the younger son experienced this certain kind of death that led to a renewal of life, but we are left wondering if the kind of death experienced by the older son ever led to a new kind of life.

Followers of Jesus are uniquely situated in place and time to help our world hear the beating heart of God. Just as this parable features a grand reversal with respect to those who were in the audience that day, so does there appear to be another kind of great reversal underway. This reversal has to do with the reality that we are beginning to see in many ways that those who have wandered in their own kind of wilderness are hearing the heartbeat of God and many of those who are planted firmly within the institutional church are tirelessly panting after the constant and unrelenting burdens and demands of the institution.

The God Pulse

This well-known parable challenges us to reframe the way that we think about prodigals. As a preliminary step in that direction, we have suggested that both sons in the parable were prodigals – they were simply prodigals in very different ways. One was a leave home kind of prodigal and the other was a stay at home kind of prodigal. One was not more or less prodigal than the other. They each had seasons in their lives where their heart did not align with their father's heart.

In moving toward a different kind of world, it will be mandatory for the people of God to be a people with a God pulse. The God pulse is so much larger than the institutional church pulse. While the institutional pulse is growing fainter by the day, the God pulse thrives in all kinds of ways throughout all kinds of people and places in our world. If we confine the God pulse to our institutional structures, programmatic mindsets, and tightly knit doctrinal statements, we are likely to miss the lifegiving heartbeat of God coursing all throughout the world.

There is nothing that a church can do to substitute for the simple mandate to love God and to love others. It is only as we walk in this kind of love that we find ourselves coming alive as people who are living in the Kingdom of God. People abandon the institutional church for a host of reasons, but at the bottom of it all is the reality that many of them can no longer find the God pulse in their church.

As communities of faith seek to engage the world, it will be essential for them to be communities where the God pulse is pursued above anything else. This means that our hearts beat for those who are far from home. Rather than building barriers that keep them far from home, we create communities that run out to welcome and receive those who had lost their way but are now coming home. We celebrate lavishly with the lost sons and daughters who have been in a far off place and have come. We don't sit in judgment of their lostness, but revel in the reality that although they were once dead, they are now alive.

It also means that those of us who have been hanging around the institutional church for some time, take an honest look at ourselves to see if we are serving merely as pawns in a powerful religious system or if we are living expressions of the life of Jesus. It is not inconceivable to imagine that some of those who have been most tightly bound to the institutional expressions of church, may in fact be some of the very ones who are furthest away from home and have the longest distance to travel to find the God pulse that God so very much desires for them to receive and celebrate.

This parable challenges us to reframe our thinking about being prodigal. While some prodigals are clearly like the younger son, other prodigals are like the older son. In whatever form it takes, we can all find what various prodigals look like by a mere gaze into the mirror. When we recognize that we are the prodigals in search of the God pulse, we can reach out to any part of the world and celebrate whomever, wherever, and whenever the God pulse finds a home in a person's life or a community of faith.

It just makes common Kingdom sense!

Step Inside

Perhaps the most overlooked feature of the Parable of the Prodigal is the make-up of the audience. There were two very defined and different groups of people – a group made up of righteous people and a group made up of unrighteous people. As you enter into this parable, identify some of the various ways in which you perceive how other groups of people relate to God. Consider also how those groups might perceive how you relate to God.

The story of the shepherd who found a lost sheep and the story of a woman who found a lost coin are stories that would have been of interest and delight to all groups of people. Identify the kinds of stories that would be of interest and delight to all groups of people in our current cultural context. What features do these particular kinds of stories have in common? How might those stories be used in telling the story of God's redemptive mission in the world?

There is a very real sense in which we are all prodigals. Some prodigals are far away from home and are fully and openly engaged in self-satisfaction. Other prodigals are much closer to home and are engaged in inner resentment and rage. Prodigals take on many forms. Reflect on how prodigal living has shown up or shows up in your life.

In what ways have you experienced God welcoming you home? In what ways can followers of Jesus and communities of faith welcome home those who are responding to God as they come to find their home in the Kingdom of God?

The word prodigal suggests such images such as "reckless living" and "wasteful spending." The word also refers to "lavish giving" and "generous bounty." Are there any ways in which this parable could actually be about a prodigal God? Consider ways that such an image might reshape our image of God or our understanding of God's mission in the world.

Chapter 7:
Totally Shrewd

"Keep smilin', keep shinin'
Knowing you can always count on me for sure
That's what friends are for
For good times and bad times
I'll be on your side forever more
That's what friends are for."

That's What Friends are For
Dionne Warwick

A Parable

There was a rich man whose manager was accused of wasting his possessions. So he called him in and asked him, "What is this I hear about you?" Give an account of your management because you cannot be manager any longer."

The manager said to himself, "What shall I do now? My master is taking away my job. I'm not strong enough to dig, and I'm ashamed to beg – I know what I'll do so, when I lose my job here, people will welcome me into their houses."

So he called in each of his master's debtors. He asked the first, "How much do you owe my master?" "Nine hundred gallons of oil," he replied. The manager told him, "Take your bill, sit down quickly, and make it four hundred and fifty."

Then he asked the second, "And how much do you owe?" "A thousand bushels of wheat," he replied. He told him, "Take your bill and make it eight hundred."

The master commended the dishonest manager because he had acted shrewdly. For the people of this world are more shrewd in dealing with their own kind than are the people of the light. I tell you, use worldly wealth to gain friends for yourselves, so that when it is gone, you will be welcomed into eternal dwellings.

Whoever can be trusted with very little can also be trusted with much, and whoever is dishonest with very little will also be dishonest with much. So, if you have not been trustworthy in handling worldly wealth, who will trust you with true riches? And if you have not been trustworthy with someone else's property, who will give you property of your own? No one can serve two masters. Either you will hate the one and love the other, or you will be devoted to the one and despise the other. You cannot serve both God and money (Luke 16:1 -13).

If any of the parables of Jesus cause us to think we have misread them, this is the one. We can hardly imagine what appears to be the clear message on the surface of the parable flowing from the lips of Jesus. Surely Jesus meant to go another direction with this parable or make another point than what seems to be obvious. Perhaps our eyes have deceived us. Surely, Jesus was not *commending* the unjust manager – he was *condemning* him. This slight adjustment to the parable would right the ship and make it possible for us to easily grasp the point.

However, there are no mistranslations that make it possible for us to wiggle out of this conundrum. The parable stands as it stands. The unjust manager got caught cooking the books of the master and Jesus commended the subsequent actions of the manager even though none of the actions taken by him were anywhere close to being consistent with the message that Jesus proclaimed. If parables are intended to pierce our minds and hearts with how the Kingdom of God functions, this parable pretty much blows a hole right through our understanding of the Kingdom of God.

The unjust manager in this story did something that would not be all that uncommon on either Wall Street or Main Street. He managed the funds of his rich boss in such a way that he could personally benefit from intentionally mismanaging the accounts. Undoubtedly, he cleverly devised a way in which his handling of the funds would be discreet. Unfortunately, his indiscretion was discovered and reported to the rich master. Upon hearing the news of his manager's mishandling of his accounts, the rich master immediately fired him and sent him on his way.

Rather than walking away from the whole matter with embarrassment and shame, the unjust manager conceived of a plan that would continue to diminish the rich master's accounts while at the same time providing financial gain and building relational capital for himself. With his pink slip looming just ahead of him, the dishonest manager went to clients and settled their debts. He accomplished this by simply asking the clients what they owed. Once the clients revealed what they owed to the rich master, the manager made an irrefusable offer – pay the debt off now at much less than what was actually owed.

Narrative Context

The Parable of the Shrewd Manager is preceded immediately by the Parable of the Prodigal Son. There is no narrative break whatsoever between these two parables. The only difference between them is the audience. The Parable of the Prodigal was directed to a group that consisted of tax collectors, sinners, Pharisees, and teachers of the Law. The Parable of the Shrewd Manager was directed only to the disciples of Jesus.

As we have seen with the case of the prodigal, the makeup of the audience plays a critical role in reading a parable. Although there is a shift in audience between these two adjacent parables, there are similarities of themes. Both parables feature characters that are responsible for resources that belong to someone else. In the Parable of the Prodigal, the younger son demanded that his portion of the inheritance be given to him. In the Parable of the Shrewd Manager, the rich man had entrusted the manager with his possessions.

Both parables also feature a primary figure without whom the parable could not be told and who is betrayed in some way. The Parable of the Prodigal has no story line without the father. Likewise, the Parable of the Shrewd Manager has no story line without the rich master. Both parables also included an element in which one of the primary characters of the story went away for an unspecified period of time. The departure and return of the younger son as well as that of the rich master were critical pieces in their respective stories. The actions taken by the younger son and those taken by the shrewd manager during the time of separation create the tension in the story line. The return of the younger son as well as the return of the rich master led to climatic moments in each parable.

Although the Parable of the Shrewd Manager was specifically aimed for the disciples of Jesus, it appears that the Pharisees overheard Jesus telling this parable and responded with sneers at Jesus' declaration at the end of the parable that it was not possible to serve both God and money. The response of the Pharisees was rooted in the reality that they were lovers of money. Undoubtedly, Jesus was well aware of their love for money and their sneers as he told this parable to his disciples. Jesus scolded the Pharisees by saying that although they justify themselves in the eyes of others, God sees their hearts.

Immediately after these two parables, Jesus went on to tell the story of another rich man who lived in luxury while a beggar named Lazarus was laid at his gate each day longing to eat the crumbs that fell from the rich man's table as the dogs licked his sores. When Lazarus died he was carried by angels to Abraham's side. When the rich man died, he was in torment and as he looked up he saw Lazarus. The rich man pleaded with Abraham to send Lazarus to him with just a drop of water on his finger to cool his tongue. Abraham reminded him that he had received good things during his life and that Lazarus had received bad things. Furthermore, there was a great chasm between Lazarus and the rich man that could not be crossed.

It is unmistakably clear that these three stories share a common thread of ways in which a concern for riches can so easily go awry. The younger son squandered his inheritance, the shrewd manager lost his job, and the rich man who disregarded Lazarus lost everything and even ended up begging for a mere drop of water. However, what turns out to be vastly more important than the riches themselves is the relationships that got twisted along the way. Although the younger son was ultimately reconciled to his father, the unjust manager did not appear to have been reconciled with the rich master.

So as not to lose sight of the larger context, all three of these stories were told as Jesus was making his way to Jerusalem where the cross was looming. As the shadow of the cross bends back against these stories, we can begin to see with greater clarity that these parables and stories were told in light of the proclamation of the Kingdom of God. Right in the middle of these stories Jesus stated that since the time of John the Baptist, the Kingdom of God was being preached and those who enter it do so by violence. This enigmatic statement about the Kingdom and violence suggests at a very rudimentary level that the Kingdom upsets and even overturns the normal order of things in our world.

Doesn't Sound Right

When the actions of the dishonest manager became known to the rich master, we might have expected for the master to declare that not only was the manager fired, he would be hanged at high noon. To our great shock, the rich master did nothing of the sort. In fact, he commended his conniving manager for coming up with and executing a shrewd plan and pulling it off right before his eyes. The rich owner was somewhat impressed by the tactics employed by his unjust manager.

The parable turns in such a way that we are almost left wondering if the rich master would have considered promoting his scandalous manager to some sort of leadership position in marketing and sales. Undoubtedly, those who were given the opportunity to pay their debts off at much lower costs would feel quite favorable toward the rich master. Since the manager had acted so shrewdly, perhaps it would be a shrewd maneuver for the rich master himself to retain such a shrewd employee. Although the parable is not concerned with whatever may have happened to the dishonest manager, the words of commendation have hung in the air for centuries.

In what world that is rooted in any sense of morality would the actions of the dishonest manager be commendable? Jesus made no effort to set the dishonest manager up as a prime example of immorality and injustice. Rather, it appears that the machinations of the manager serve as a very thought provoking way for Jesus to transition to what it means to be stewards of the gifts of God in the Kingdom. Just as the manager figured out how to leverage a difficult situation in order to make friends, what would it look like for those of us who follow Jesus to leverage the gifts that God has given us to be as shrewd in the light as the dishonest manager was in the dark?

The Shrewd Deed

A rich master leaving his home for an extended and unspecified amount of time while leaving a manager to oversee his business affairs is not particularly uncommon for the rich. It is likewise not all that uncommon for there to be some form of mismanagement that happens in the process. In this particular scene, a manager had been accused of wasting his rich master's possessions. Upon hearing what the manager had been doing, the rich master wasted no time in calling him in to give an account. The rich master did not call the manager in to give an account so that he might have a chance to justify his actions and save his job. He was called in because he was losing his job.

There appears to be no path by which the dishonest manager could save his job. In the parable, he made no attempt whatsoever to justify his actions or beg for mercy in order to keep his job. Rather, his thoughts went immediately to what actions he could take to protect and preserve his own well-being. He admitted to himself that he did not have the stamina and will for physical labor and that he was too proud to beg.

The only path that the manager could see in moving forward so that his basic life's needs could be met was by reimagining his former clients in terms of new friends. With one last gasp of business shrewdness, the manager went to the clients and simply offered them the forgiveness of their remaining debt if they could but pay a reduced portion of it off on that very day. The terms of such a proposition would be naturally irresistible for any person who owed a debt. The shrewdness lies not only in the fact that debtors received a receipt of paid in full while only actually paying in part, but in the fact that the unjust manager was able to leverage business transactions to create a friendship base. He shrewdly transferred the indebtedness of the clients from the rich man to himself.

This savvy maneuver of transforming business clients into friends was so well conceived and executed that the rich master commended the dishonest manager for his shrewdness. Although the accounts of the rich master suffered loss through these transactions, there was no way that he could deny how brilliantly they were conducted. Given the circumstances in which all this transpired, the rich master simply could not find a way to condemn the actions taken by his unjust manager in the way that he resolved the debts of the clients and created friends along the way.

Ethical Anxiety

From the time this parable was recorded, it has been the source of some angst and anxiety among faithful readers of Scripture. Jesus clearly controlled the terms of the parable. This was not a news account or a story that happened among the elite living in Jerusalem. It was simply a story told in the form of a parable in which Jesus had complete control of all the levers. Perhaps there was no great surprise in that the rich master would commend his unjust manager for the way in which he dealt with the debts owed to this rich master. The master could clearly see the cleverness of it all and perhaps the only words left to say were, "Well done, my skilled and faithless manager."

We can almost hear those same words coming from Jesus. In no way did Jesus condemn the actions of the unjust manager. Our expectation might be that Jesus would blast the actions of the manager and make it crystal clear that under no circumstances would such behavior be acceptable. This would have been a great opportunity for Jesus to talk about the fiery pit of hell and the eternal torture awaiting the dishonest manager and those who conducted business in the same kind of way that he did.

However, Jesus chose a different path. He threw his hat in the ring with the rich master and stated that the people of this world are more shrewd in dealing with those who walk in darkness than are the people of the light are in dealing with those who walk in the light. In this way, the shrewd manager was something of a shining example for those who are of the darkness of this world.

Jesus did, in fact, go on to say that those who could be trusted with very little could be trusted with much and that those who were dishonest with little would be dishonest with much. Furthermore, those who have not been trustworthy with worldly wealth, could not be trusted with true riches. All of this came to a resounding conclusion – "No one can serve two masters (Luke 16:13)."

When we take a step back from the parable it becomes a little more clear what Jesus is saying. Jesus is not using this parable to promote immoral or unethical measures as a means of creating friends who can be there in our time of need. Rather, he used this parable to mirror the reality that those who work in the darkness outperform those who work in the light. Jesus was not suggesting that those who live in light are to mirror the activities of those who live in the dark. He is simply saying that those who live in the dark do a better job at living in the dark than those who live in the light do at living in the light.

Stewardship and Ownership

This parable ultimately rests on a very significant misstep made by the unjust manager. The fact that he turned out to be unjust was a symptom of a deeper problem. He was charged by the rich master to serve as the steward of his possessions until his return. The manager was entrusted to manage the possessions of the rich man in a manner that would be fully consistent with the way the rich master would have managed them if he had been there. The fundamental purpose of the manager was to act in the best interests of his rich master. He was entrusted with the possessions of his master as if they were his very own.

However, in his responsibility as manager he began to assume some of the possessions as if he were the owner rather than the manager. At some point in time, he began to act in his own interest rather than the interest of his rich master. In so doing, he breached his responsibility of management and drifted over into ownership. This kind of drift may seem small on paper, but in real life it represents a seismic shift. As stewards we recognize that someone else is the author, creator, or owner of certain products, possessions, or ideas. Faithful and trustworthy stewards are called upon to execute the wishes and desires of those who have placed their trust in them.

At the point where the stewards or managers no longer serve that purpose, they can no longer be deemed trustworthy and faithful. When the interests of the manager are no longer aligned with those for whom they manage, those interests will eventually emerge. There is no way to keep the lid on when the steward loses sight of what or for whom they are stewarding. At some point the divergence in interests between the parties involved becomes too great to go unnoticed. It was this kind of divergence that came to the attention of the rich master in the parable and prompted him to ask his manager to give an account of his stewardship.

This is actually a reflection of what happened in the Garden of Eden. God created the most wonderful place for Adam and Eve to cultivate. They were placed in the garden to serve as the stewards of God's creation. It was the perfect set up. As part of their stewardship, they were commanded to multiply and be fruitful. Another part of their stewardship was that they were not to eat the fruit of the tree of the knowledge of good and evil. The command to not eat of the fruit was not because the fruit itself was poisonous or that having knowledge of good and evil was bad. The command to not eat of the fruit of that particular tree was rooted in the reality that the knowledge of good and evil represented a shift from stewardship to that of ownership. Rather than stewarding the gift of creation that God had given to them, Adam and Eve sought to be like God – who alone was the creator.

Kingdom Stewards

Most of us have been raised in cultures in which we value such things as ownership of personal possessions. These are often the very things that are used to measure our success or worth. As we have seen in previous parables, there is nothing inherently wrong with possessions themselves. A nice house or luxurious car is simply that – a nice house or a luxurious car. In and of themselves, they function in the same way as money. The evil is not in the money itself, but in the way that money shapes us and impacts our actions and relationships.

When things went sideways in the Garden of Eden as Adam and Eve ate the fruit from the tree of the knowledge of good and evil, it was the relationships that suffered the initial onslaught of the death that was promised for eating the fruit. Heavy damage was done in the realm of every conceivable relationship – even the relationship between humanity and creation itself. The damage done in every direction was so devastating that God ultimately washed the earth clean and started a "new" creation story with Noah and his family.

The Noah story did not go exceptionally well either and ended in its own fiasco of people who wanted to build a tower to heaven. Rather than washing the earth as he did with the flood, God scattered the people by confusing the languages. He would eventually create a new group of people whom he would bless so that the world would be blessed through them. God's desire for the world to be blessed through Abraham and his family was also reflected in the previous parable about the farmer and his bumper crop of grain.

The current that runs through both of these parables has to do with stewardship in terms of recognizing the difference between what is given to us as a gift from God for the purpose of blessing others and what we claim as our own possession to bless ourselves. There is so much confusion about how followers relate to possessions, that a number of savvy religious leaders have succeeded in leveraging the confusion in ways that build up their bank accounts and empires while leaving many impoverished givers with the false hope that if they had faith, they too would experience the fruit that grows from sowing dollars here and planting seeds there.

The story of the unjust steward provides a mirror in which we all see ourselves as somewhat warped and self-seeking when it comes to managing the gifts that God has given us – we quickly move from stewarding the gifts in ways that bless the world to possessing the gifts in ways that satisfy our own appetites. Once we have eaten the forbidden fruit, it is hard to go back from where we came. Even though the unjust manager could go back to all the previous clients of the rich master, he had to go back in a way that allowed him to create very different kinds of relationships. It is in this moment that we see his commendable shrewdness.

Leveraging in the Light

The unjust manager did an amazing job of leveraging the darkness in a world of darkness. He did it so well, he was commended for it by the rich master and Jesus used him as a positive example for those who live in the light. Jesus did not call on those who live in the light to steal or embezzle from their employers or to cheat in their business dealings. But he did call followers to be as shrewd about living in the light as the unjust manager was about living in the dark. From Jesus' perspective, those who live in the light had not quite caught up with the kind of shrewdness exhibited by those living in the dark. Jesus was telling this parable to point out that there appeared to be no one in the light whose shrewdness was a match for that of the unjust manager.

This parable challenges us to learn how to leverage relationships in light of seeing ourselves as stewards of God's gifts in the world. When we relax the grip of ownership, we can then truly receive and share the gift of stewardship. This is what it means to live with shrewdness in the light. This kind of shrewdness does not rely on manipulation or control seeking measures to gain favorable relational outcomes in times of desperation. In other words, shrewdness in the light does not use people to advance our personal agendas.

When things like possessions, wealth, and assets are not our life focus, then we can be open to the kind of stewardship that values relationships – whether they are relationships with other people, our relationship with God, our relationship with creation, or even our relationship with ourselves. What Jesus staked down in the parable was that we cannot love the things of the dark and the things of the light at the same time. Once we drive down our own stake, what we love and hate will be openly revealed.

Moving from the strongholds of ownership to the strength and courage of stewardship is a huge step in our world. As the followers of Jesus move forward, we must increase our footprint of being faithful stewards in the world as we abandon the effort to relate to wealth and possessions with the same kind of shrewdness that is used of those who live in the dark. We are called to live by a different kind of shrewdness – one that befits those who live in the light. The Son of Man had nowhere to lay his head, yet he lived in the full light and freedom of being a faithful steward over what he himself created.

The stewardship issue has been primarily co-opted by the financial issues related to the institutional church. When it is announced that a steward sermon, a stewardship series, or a stewardship campaign will be conducted, every single person knows that this is about the money. This very slim vision of stewardship has skewed the much larger vision of stewardship and has in fact robbed us of the joy and freedom of thinking about stewardship in terms of the all the gifts God has given us to be stewards of.

Reclaiming a thoroughly biblical and deeply theological vision of stewardship not only transforms us, it transforms the world in which we live. Our shrewdness of stewardship should be no less than the kind of shrewdness practiced in the world. As our practice of Kingdom shrewdness continues to push against the darkness, our witness and mission in the world will have far greater power and much deeper impact.

It just makes common Kingdom sense!

Step Inside

Parables inherently have shock value. This is one of the primary reasons that Jesus spoke in parables. The Kingdom of God is not a casual conversation about a theological theme. It is a living reality that confronts us on our own terms. On its surface, The Parable of the Shrewd Manager seems to have gotten it wrong. Reflect on some of your own initial reactions in reading this parable.

Our current culture is strongly founded on notions of ownership. We often measure our place and success in life in terms of things that we own or have the potential to own. At its heart, stewardship is about recognizing that we are the stewards and managers of things ranging from money and personal possessions to our attitudes and relationships. Stewardship speaks to our entire life – being stewards is in fact a *way* of life. Consider some of the ways in which this parable speaks to your own practices of ownership and stewardship.

One of the most remarkable features of this parable was Jesus suggesting that those who live in the dark do a better job of living in the dark than those who live in the light do of living in the light. What might be some of the ways in which you see this observation played out in the context of your community of faith?

In this parable, the shrewd manager experienced a significant life crises. The things that he managed were more important than the people who were impacted by his management. After the return of his master and the loss of his job, the manager began to see that the true value of his job was the very people that he had "shrewd" over. Reflect on an experience in your own life or community of faith when other ambitions got in the way of the people we were called to serve, love, and bless.

Chapter 8:
Ceiling Prayers

"Yes, and how many times must a man look up
Before he can see the sky?
And how many ears must one man have
Before he can hear people cry?
Yes, and how many deaths will it take 'til he knows
That too many people have died?

The answer, my friend, is blowin' in the wind
The answer is blowin' in the wind."

Blowing in the Wind
Bob Dylan

A Parable or Two

In a certain town there was a judge who neither feared nor cared what people thought. And there was a widow in that town who kept coming to him with the plea, "Grant me justice against my adversary." For some time, he refused. But finally, he said to himself, "Even though I don't fear God or care what people think, yet because this widow keeps bothering me, I will see that she gets justice, so that she won't eventually come and attack me!"

And the Lord said, "Listen to what the unjust judge says. And will not God bring about justice for his chosen ones, who cry out to him day and night? Will he keep putting them off? I tell you, he will see that they get justice, and quickly. However, when the Son of Man comes, will he find faith on the earth (Luke 18: 1 – 8)?"

Two men went up to the Temple to pray, one a Pharisee and the other a tax collector. The Pharisee stood by himself and prayed: "God, I thank you that I am not like other people – robbers, evildoers, adulterers – or even like this tax collector. I fast twice a week and give a tenth of all I get."

But the tax collector stood at a distance. He would not even look up to heaven, but beat his breast and said, "God, have mercy on me, a sinner." I tell you that this man, rather than the other, went home justified before God. For all those who exalt themselves will be humbled, and those who humble themselves will be exalted (Luke 18:10 – 14).

These two parables dealing with prayer are placed right up against each other. The only thing separating them are Luke's brief words that the second parable was specifically addressed to those who were confident in their own righteousness and looked down on everyone else. The first parable had been directed to Jesus' disciples. Both parables address the theme of prayer. The shift of audience gives each parable its own character and different cast of characters altogether.

In the first parable, a widow keeps appearing before a judge with the same request for justice. As a widow she had undoubtedly been marginalized by the community and most likely struggled to support herself. Although it is not known what the particular claim was that she was repeatedly making before the judge, it is clear that there was an adversary who had committed an injustice against her

The widow's pleas were not resolved for some time. This was not because she did not have a just case but because the judge was not a man who cared about God or about what anyone else thought about him. After repeated attempts by the widow to be heard, the unjust judge eventually addressed her plea. He did not grant her justice out of a sense of justice itself, but out of a sense of being worn down by her constant request and the nearly inexplicable fear that she would come and attack him. He simply responded because he no longer wished to be bothered.

Jesus then compared the response of the unjust judge to this widow to the response of God to those who belong to him. When God's people cry out, God will hear them immediately and bring about justice swiftly. God will not put off the pleas and prayers of his people. The first parable then concluded with Jesus asking if the Son of Man will find faith on the earth upon his arrival.

The subsequent parable maintained the focus on prayer but goes off in an entirely different direction. In this parable, a Pharisee and a tax collector went to the Temple to pray. The Pharisee stood by himself and prayed a prayer of thankfulness that he was not like other people such as robbers, adulterers, evil doers, nor even like the tax collector who had also come to pray. The Pharisee informed God that he also fasted twice a week and was a faithful tither.

In contrast to the Pharisee, the tax collector stood at a distance. He could not even bear to look up to heaven. He beat his chest as he prayed for God to have mercy on him as a sinner. Jesus stated that the tax collector – rather than the Pharisee – was the one who went home as being justified before God. He concluded the parable with the saying that all those who exalt themselves will be humbled, and those who humble themselves will be exalted.

Narrative Context

These back to back parables are set clearly in the context of Jesus' final journey to Jerusalem. The geographical markers on each side of the parables are essential to the movement of the story line. Prior to the parables, it was reported that as Jesus was heading toward Jerusalem that he traveled along the border between Samaria and Galilee. As he was entering a village, ten lepers stood off at a distance and called out to him to have pity on them. Jesus commanded them to go show themselves to the priests.

As the lepers made their way to the priests, they were all cleansed. However, only one of them came back praising God. This cleansed leper – a Samaritan – threw himself down at Jesus' feet and thanked him. Jesus asked why the other nine who had also been cleansed and who were Jews had not come back to do what this one foreigner had done.

The geographical marker after the parables notes that Jesus was approaching Jericho. As he neared the city, he encountered a blind man who was sitting and begging along the side of the road. Asking as to why there was such a streaming crowd, the blind man was told that Jesus of Nazareth was passing by. Just as the lepers had, the blind man cried out for mercy. When Jesus asked him what he wanted, the blind man declared that he wanted to see. Immediately he received his sight and began to follow Jesus.

Along with geographical markers on each side of these two parables, there is also a poignant story about a rich man on either side of the parables. Prior to the parables is the story of Lazarus and the rich man – which we noted in the last chapter as a story which also served as a bookend to the Parable of the Shrewd Manager. The Parable of the Rich Man and Lazarus also serves as a set up for the two prayer parables.

A story of a rich man resurfaces on the other side of the prayer parables as a certain rich ruler approached Jesus and asked what he must do to have eternal life. Although he had faithfully kept the law from childhood, Jesus told him that he was lacking just one thing. In order to follow Jesus, he would need to sell everything that he had and give it to the poor. Seeing the sadness of the rich man, Jesus observed that it was easier for a camel to go through the eye of a needle than for a rich person to enter the Kingdom of God.

Flowing immediately out of the two parables on prayer is a story of people who were bringing their babies to Jesus to put his hands on them. The disciples rebuked the people, but Jesus called the children to himself and commanded that they not be forbidden from coming to him for the Kingdom of God belongs to such as them. He further stated that one must receive the Kingdom of God like a child in order to enter it.

The cluster of stories surrounding the two prayer parables are focused on various groups of people who live on the margins and shadows of social and community life. Along with those we have already mentioned – Lazarus the beggar, the ten lepers, little children, and the blind beggar – there is also a character in each of the prayer parables that would be considered among the outcasts – a widow and a tax collector.

The Relentless Widow

A certain widow in a certain town was the unfortunate victim of an adversary who had committed an injustice against her. The particulars concerning the loss of her husband or the kind of injustice that had been committed against her are unknown. The only thing that is known for certain is that she had an indomitable spirit and she would not give up her quest for having a wrong made right.

The obstacle that this widow faced in seeking justice was not that it was a frivolous and inconsequential matter, but that the judge simply did not care about God and people. His care did not extend beyond the reach of his own life – anything beyond that mattered little to him. It was of no concern to him that this widow had a just cause and needed his help to make things right. Since she was a widow, he most likely disregarded her altogether and saw her as having no possible means of being a benefit to his personal welfare in any way whatsoever.

The only possible strategy available to this widow was to keep showing up at the judge's door. She undoubtedly came to know that he would not respond to her as a person or to the injustice that had been committed against her by her adversary. The only way into his life was for her to become such a pesky nuisance to him that it best served his interests to deal with her ceaseless persistence. Her persistence was so strongly felt that at some point the uncaring judge feared that she might assault him physically. She had to disrupt his self-interest to the point that he had to relieve himself of her.

The Wrong Idea

On its face, it may appear that the point of the parable is that God deals with issues of justice when we are persistent enough to get his attention or wear him down. The uncaring judge simply conceded to the persistence of the widow. It was not as if it finally occurred to him that she had a case that needed to be heard or a wrong that needed to be righted. Like ceaseless drops of water from a leaky faucet, her persistence broke him.

If we are not careful, we could easily draw the wrong conclusion. Our image of God could be skewed in such a way as to think of prayer as a tool that we can use to wear God down to the point that he will concede. This would be a tragic and exhausting mental image of God to sustain in our minds and hearts. It would be a gross misrepresentation to think that because there is so much injustice, pain, and brokenness in the world that God does not care or is not involved in such matters. It would be a burden far too heavy to bear if we imagined that we had to pray God into submission to do what is right, just and loving.

The purpose of the parable is not to instruct us to pound away at God until his dull ears and hard heart are so penetrated by our deep cries that he simply concedes in order to get us to stop. After concluding the parable, Jesus in fact went on to depict God as *not* being like the uncaring judge. God does not have to be coerced into bringing about justice for his own people. He is not pressed into submission by our constant pleas for righting the vast wrongs of the world – he is already far ahead of us in doing just that.

Could it be that the point of the parable all along was not so much about us seeking to get God to do something that he was unwilling to do, but to invite us to share in what God is already doing? The point of persistence is not so much to move God as it is to move us. We are the ones who are profoundly changed by crying out to God. Praying does not make God love us more. Rather, it opens our hearts so that we have greater capacity to love God more. The purpose of prayer is not to bend God toward our will, but for our will to bend toward God's will. We are not like widows seeking to break an uncaring judge – we are children who are more cared for than we can even imagine.

The Wrong Prayer

What could be more soul shaking than learning that the most righteous people we know are praying the wrong prayer? In the second parable, Jesus fashioned the stories of two men who went to the Temple area to pray. The first man was steeped in a kind of religious righteousness that he had worked hard to procure. His status as an exceptionally righteous person was known to any who knew him or who even knew of him.

The very fact that he stood by himself to pray was a sure sign that he was set apart from all others who came to the Temple area to pray. He was a religious standout whose prayer of self-adulation said it all. Nothing further needed to be said apart from the visual display that he was not like everybody else. His religious status as a Pharisee had bumped him far ahead of the rest of humanity. His prayer was simply a "humble" reminder to everyone else, to himself, and even to God, that he was all alone in his own world of self-righteousness.

In contrast, there was another man who stood off by himself. He did so not because he thought of himself as being righteous in any way, but because he knew there was not a shred of righteousness to be found in him. His own sense of *righteouslessness* was so deeply profound that he beat his chest as he prayed. This tax collector was so burdened by his guilt and shame he could not even lift his head to heaven. He stood at a distance not to put on a show but because he was so disconnected from God that he dared not seek to occupy the sacred space of the Pharisee.

The tax collector was also a publicly known figure. He most certainly could feel the hard stares and the deep hatred of all those who saw him and had been swindled and burned by his by his burdensome demands. Yet, his heavy hands which once received the taxes of the people were now beating against his own body. All the collection of coins in the world could not rid him of the reality that his soul was bankrupt. The many pleas for mercy that he had received as he collected the taxes of the people, were now the words that passed over his very own lips.

On the Margins

These two prayer parables feature two very different people whose only commonality was that they lived on the margins. They were ostracized for very different reasons. The widow had few resources and no advocates for her cause. The tax collector had an abundance of resources at his disposal and could make demands of the people at will. Both of them, however, lived outside of the mainstream of Jewish community. In their own separate ways, they were both bankrupt.

A central concern for marginalized people is who they have access to. The very fact that they are marginalized suggests that their access to certain people or resources is restricted. The widow was pounding the door of the one she needed access to and the tax collector was pounding his chest as he cried out before God. Both of them were pleading for the mere mercy to be heard and for wrongs to be made right.

These two parables are not just a couple of parables on prayer, they are parables that speak to the issue of who has access to God. Neither the widow nor the tax collector would have been given much chance of having access to the one to whom they cried out. Mainstream society would have written off any hope that the widow would be heard by a judge – especially an uncaring judge. Not only was she heard, justice was rendered.

Likewise, nobody from the religious elite – especially Pharisees – would have thought that the tax collector would have any chance of receiving mercy from a God whose wrath was turned toward the wicked. The tax collector had not only robbed others, he had robbed God and now hoped that somehow his cry for forgiveness would be granted just because he dared to approach God and plea for mercy.

As Jesus was nearing Jerusalem, it should have been clear that this was no time for marginalized people to have access to him. The business at hand was far too serious for the unnecessary interruptions of naïve children, the justice concerns of widows, or the cries for mercy from tax collectors. Yet, these two parables are joined at the hip as they each tell their story from such very different contexts. The marginalized are not alone. Those who lived in the shadowlands had full access to the living God whose mercy extended far beyond the borders of human boundaries.

Gaining Access

Much of our lives has to do with gaining access to people, resources, opportunities, institutions, and other entities. The institutional church has for a very long time played a religious role in who gets access to what. This includes such things as who gets access to religious leaders, who can participate in religious rites, who's voice is heard among the religious elite, and who gets to be part of the religious community.

There is even the very important determination of who gets access to God – or to heaven itself. The keys to access may not be literal, but the costs associated with getting access to people, things, or services under the reign of religious institutionalism can be quite high. For some, these costs may be overwhelming and formidable.

Many people are not associated with a religious institution or community because they have on far too many occasions experienced the unwritten rules of the institution or have wisely sized up the televangelist of the day and know that at the end of the show there is a price to be paid. There is no shortage of religious gatekeepers who influence – or even control – the access points to all things religious.

As followers of Jesus and communities of faith, we have a grand opportunity to facilitate the journey of people from all walks of life as they yearn for something more fulfilling than the unlimited numbers of connections they can have through a boat load of social media platforms. What many seem to be hoping for is that if they can make a certain number of connections with certain people, they can find purpose and meaning in life. Somewhere in the quest of it all there is the faint hope that they will experience a sense of validation or self-worth.

The reality is that there is not a magical number of connections which can be made that transforms our search for meaning into the experience of meaning. Things like meaning, purpose, and self-worth are not rooted in the number of connections we make, but in the One who made us to be connected.

We already have a world longing for connectivity, we simply need to facilitate and cultivate what God is already doing in people's lives so that they can begin to engage and embrace a personal relationship with the living God who desires for them to experience the abundance of life itself – not just the stuff that we find along the way through life.

For a limitless variety of reasons, many people do not feel that they have access to God. In the sense that none of us experience freedom of forgiveness and wholeness without a relationship with God, we are all marginalized. Whether we are more like the widow or the tax collector, we all stand somewhere along the spectrum of marginalization and pray one way or the other that God will hear us and grant us the great gift of access.

One of the easiest, and yet most profound ways, for followers of Jesus to facilitate access to God for our world is to provide the world with access to us. The world is no longer a "Come to our church" or "All are welcome" kind of world. These statements and sentiments do next to nothing to convey to those who feel that they do not have access to God that they do in fact have access to God.

The notion of making ourselves accessible to the world was supremely revealed in the incarnation of Jesus himself. The incarnation refers not only to his birth – it refers to his entire life as the embodiment of God among us. Accessibility is all about presence. God was fully present in Jesus, and Jesus was fully present in our world. In other words, God was fully accessible through the presence of Jesus.

When we as followers of Jesus make ourselves accessible to the world, we are facilitating the journeys of countless numbers of people who are seeking to be connected to God. This is not the same thing as making our churches and church programs accessible to any who might come. This is the church living outside of its institutional life to be present in the world as the ongoing incarnation and expression of Jesus empowered by the Spirit of God. Our constant and ever present enfleshment of the Living Lord in our world bears faithful and fruitful witness that all people have access to God and that God has made himself accessible to all.

It just makes common Kingdom sense!

Step Inside

These two parables feature individuals who are seeking to gain access to someone who can make things right. The widow repeatedly seeks access to the judge and the tax collector begs for mercy as he seeks access to God. Those watching the plights of each of these individuals could easily conclude that the widow would have little chance of gaining access to the judge and the tax collector would have little chance of gaining access to God. Reflect on experiences in your own life where you were denied access to something or someone that you were seeking access to.

The persistent return of the widow to the judge's house and the continuous beating of the tax collector upon his own chest as they each seek to gain access, could paint a very skewed picture of what it is like to gain access to God. In what ways might these two parables represent our misguided notions or attempts to have access to God?

The story of Jesus focuses on the coming of God to our world through the fleshly and living presence of Jesus. The incarnation of Jesus refers not only to his birth story, but to his entire story of being God in the flesh among us. The church is intended to be an ongoing enfleshment of the presence of Jesus in the world. In what ways as followers of Jesus and communities of faith do we embody the message of free access to God by all people?

Chapter 9:
Meanwhile

"Here comes the sun, doo-doo-doo-doo
Here comes the sun, and I say
It's alright

Little darlin', it's been a long, cold, lonely winter
Little darlin', it feels like years since it's been here

Here comes the sun, doo-doo-doo-doo
Here comes the sun, and I say
It's alright."

Here Comes the Sun
The Beatles

A Parable

A man of noble birth went to a distant country to have himself appointed king and then to return. So he called ten of his servants and gave them minas. "Put this money to work," he said, "until I come back." But his subjects hated him and sent a delegation after him to say, "We don't want this man to be our king."

He was made king, however, and returned home. Then he sent for the servants to whom he had given the money, in order to find out what they had gained with it. The first came and said, "Sir, your mina has earned ten more." "Well done, my good servant!" his master replied. "Because you have been trustworthy in a very small matter, take charge of ten cities."

The second came and said, "Sir, your mina has earned five more." His master answered, "You take charge of five cities." Then another servant came and said, "Sir, here is your mina; I kept it laid away in a piece of cloth. I was afraid of you because you are a hard man. You take out what you did not put in and reap what you did not sow."

His master replied, "I will judge you by your own words, you wicked servant! You knew, did you, that I am a hard man, taking out what I did not put in, and reaping what I did not sow? Why then didn't you put my money on deposit, so that when I came back, I could have collected it with interest?" Then he said to those standing by, "Take his mina away from him and give it to the one who has ten minas."

"Sir," they said, "he already has ten!" He replied, "I tell you that to everyone who has, more will be given, but as for the one who has nothing, even what they have will be taken away. But those enemies of mine who did not want me to be king over them – bring them here and kill them in front of me (Luke 19: 12 – 27)."

This parable represents the final parable in the travelogue journey of Jesus as he made his way to Jerusalem for the grand finale of the cross and resurrection. In the event that this parable sounded slightly off to you, it is most likely because the same parable appears in the Gospel of Matthew in a slightly different way. Matthew's version features three servants who received various amounts of *talents* according to their abilities. The servants were given five, two, and one talent respectively. The servants with five and two talents doubled the amount of talents originally given to them. The servant with one talent hid it in the ground and presented it back to the master upon his return.

In Luke's version of the parable, a single *mina* was given to each of ten servants. However, Luke only recorded the experiences of three of the servants. Similarly to Matthew's version, two of the servants presented their mina back with interest and one did not. One servant turned his mina into ten minas, another servant turned his mina into five minas, and the third servant folded his mina in a cloth and hid it away until the master returned as a newly appointed king.

In both parables, the servants who turned investments on their talents or minas were generously rewarded by the master. The one servant in each parable that failed to return their talent or mina without interest were scolded for their laziness and wickedness. Not only would their one talent or mina be taken away from them, they would be turned over to the most horrific of fates including death.

Luke's parable of the minas is the capstone parable of Jesus' journey to Jerusalem. Immediately after telling this parable, Jesus continued the last part of his journey and came to the Mount of Olives. From there he sent two of his disciples into a village to procure a colt which had never been ridden. When the colt was brought back to Jesus, he rode through the town as crowds lined the roads and broke forth in open praise of Jesus as the king who comes in the name of the Lord.

Narrative Context

This parable flows immediately from the various stories of those who were considered to be outsiders in Jewish community life. These would include such groups as children, rich rulers, the blind, the poor, and tax collectors. These are the same stories which flowed from the two parables on prayer that we considered in the previous chapter.

The story of Zacchaeus is told immediately prior to the Parable of the Minas. Zacchaeus was the chief tax collector and had become quite rich from exorbitant taxes paid by the Jewish people. When news hit the streets that Jesus was coming through Jericho, Zacchaeus wanted to see Jesus. However, because of his small physical stature, he could not see over the crowds of people. Zacchaeus ran ahead of the crowd and climbed into a sycamore tree.

When Jesus passed by the tree in which Zacchaeus was perched, he told him to come down immediately. Zacchaeus came down from the tree and gladly welcomed Jesus. As they made their way to Zacchaeus' house, the crowd began to mutter that Jesus was going to the house of a sinner. During Jesus' stay at Zacchaeus house, Zacchaeus boldly confessed that he would give half of his possessions to the poor and would give four times the amount to any whom he had cheated. Jesus replied to Zacchaeus that salvation had come to his house because he too was a son of Abraham. Jesus then announced his mission of coming to seek and save the lost.

The story of Zacchaeus opens the door to give us a first-hand glimpse of what it looks like when the son of Abraham and the Son of God end up in the same house. We get one of the clearest pictures yet of the effect of salvation. As Zacchaeus sat in the tree to get a look at Jesus, he was undoubtedly also looking over all the other people in the crowd from whom he exacted his wealth. He could also see the poor and needy and be reminded of the burden they were to the rest of the community. When Zacchaeus experienced the salvation that came to his house that day, he was filled with a very different kind of vision for those whom he had so egregiously taxed as well as those for whom he held such deep contempt.

Zacchaeus' experience also opens the door for us to see what salvation looks like as it played out in the parable of the minas. The Son of Man had given one mina each to ten sons of Abraham. While he was away, some invested their minas and have even more to present to the master when he returned as king, while others chose to place their mina in safe keeping to be presented back to him upon his arrival. Those who invested their minas were used as a depiction of the dynamic energy of salvation. The one who did not invest his mina was used as a depiction of laziness and fruitlessness. One scene depicted the dynamic energy of salvation as it works each day to gain interest. The end result for the one who did not invest their mina was not only the loss of their only mina, but the loss of salvation itself.

An Allusion

The Parable of the Minas encompassed an historical allusion that would be well remembered by the Jews. As Jesus and his entourage made their way from Jericho to Jerusalem, the disciples anticipated that Jesus would reveal himself as the Messiah in Jerusalem and that the Kingdom of God would gloriously appear. However, the parable depicted a narrative that was somewhat different than what the disciples imagined.

Jesus told the story of a nobleman who went off to a far country to receive the kingdom. Many who knew the nobleman were opposed to him being crowned king and ruler over them. The opposition ran so deep that a delegation was even sent to oppose the crowning of the nobleman. The story actually alludes to the attempt of Archelaus, the son of Herod the Great, to be crowned king by none other than the Caesar himself. After the death of his father, Archelaus made a journey to Rome for just that purpose. Although Archelaus was hated by many over whom he was lord, Caesar crowned him king and sent him back to rule over half of the kingdom once ruled by Herod the Great.

The Come Back King

The historical backdrop sets the stage for the eschatological framing of this parable. The similarities between the story of Archelaus, the landowner in the parable, and that of Jesus begin to align. The parable looks back to the Archelaus story and ahead to the Jesus story. Jesus' arrival in Jerusalem was not to establish his reign in the manner in which his disciples thought. Rather, the journey to Jerusalem was part of a larger journey in which he would eventually go away with the promise of coming back – just as Archelaus did some thirty years before and the landowner did in the parable.

All three stories share an interest in what happened in the "in between time" of the leaving of the would be king and the return of the newly crowned king. In all three stories, there was a significant part of the population that stood in opposition to these respective individuals and to the notion that they would return to reign over them. In fact, whether it is the historical allusion, the parabolic reference, or the eschatological expectation, energetic but futile efforts were made by those who stood in opposition to thwart the would be kings and their respective kingdoms.

It is what happens during the "in between times" that is of importance in the parable. On the one hand there were some who sought to thwart the crowning of the rich landowner. On the other hand, there were ten servants who had been commanded to put the minas that had been given to them to work. The rich landowner was made king and promptly returned home. When he got back home, he sent for the ten servants to whom he had given the ten minas.

The first servant had earned ten more minas. The second servant earned five more minas. A third servant had securely wrapped his mina in a cloth and stored it away because of his fear of the harshness of the master. The master placed the first servant in charge of ten cities. He then placed the second servant in charge of five cities. The first servant was commended for being faithful in a few things. Apart from placing him in charge of five cities, the master said nothing further to the second servant. The master then ordered that the mina of the third servant be taken away and given to the servant who had ten minas.

An Objection

When the master ordered that the mina of the servant who brought back one be taken away and given to the servant who already had ten minas, there arose an objection from those who were standing by. The objection was not that the one and only mina from one servant was taken from him, but that it was given to the servant with ten minas. Undoubtedly, the popular feeling among the bystanders was that the mina should have been given to someone who had none. To add further drama to the story, the master then ordered for everyone who had been in opposition to him becoming king to be brought before him and killed in his very presence.

The finale of this parable has a certain harshness about it that may be disconcerting to us. Not only did the master give the mina to the servant who already had ten, he even promised more for those who had more and less for those who had nothing. This would not easily agree with notions of justice and fairness. The killing off of the king's opponents certainly does not seem to align with the mandate of Jesus to love even our enemies.

The conclusion to this parable could push any of us over the cliff of biblical interpretation. Just moments earlier, Jesus had announced that salvation had come to the home of Zacchaeus and the crowds that had followed Jesus as he neared Jerusalem had assumed that the Kingdom was about to appear at once.

In great measure, this parable was told by Jesus to speak to our short-sighted and mistaken views concerning the Kingdom of God. After Jesus had spoken the parable, he went on to Jerusalem where he would be welcomed as a king as he entered the city. Upon entering Jerusalem, he wept for the city and announced that the day was coming when their enemies would surround the city and dash the inhabitants – including children – to the ground. Not one stone would be left upon another, because they did not recognize the timing of God's coming.

When Jesus entered the Temple courts, he began to drive out all those who were selling and declared that they had turned a house of prayer into a den of thieves and robbers. As he taught daily at the Temple the chief priests, teachers of the law, and leaders of the people sought to kill him but could not find a way to do so because the people were hanging on his every word.

When the parable of the minas is seen as the connector between the salvation that had come to the home of Zacchaeus and the judgment that had already begun to unfold at the Temple with Jesus's arrival, we just might hear this parable in a slightly different way. As in all cases of biblical interpretation, the larger context helps us to better navigate the text before us.

A Renewed Eschatology

Eschatology is often a divisive and complicated biblical subject. It has started many theological wars and taken more prisoners than any of us would wish. However, at its very heart, eschatology is rooted in the Kingdom of God. Without a Kingdom, there would be no eschatological discourse to worry about.

This parable of Jesus is placed exactly where it is because it addresses the eschatological misconceptions of both the religious leaders who stood in opposition to Jesus as well as the misconceptions of the crowds of people who lined the streets to welcome him to Jerusalem.

Neither group had a grasp of eschatology in which they understood that the Kingdom of God had already been initiated with the inaugural event of Jesus' ministry and would be consummated by another coming to Jerusalem – but not this coming.

There was also a basic misperception about the nature of the messiah that would bring about the Kingdom of God. Although Jesus fulfilled the function of God's messiah, he was not the *kind* of messiah that had been expected. He came without an army and certainly did not seek to overthrow the mighty empire of the Romans. There were no indications that he was planning to overthrow the politically powerful Caesar and usurp his throne.

There were also no expectations that Jesus would be a suffering servant *kind* of messiah. Yet, it was this very reality about him that defined his messiahship. Getting a better grasp of the *kind* of messiah Jesus was directly impacts the *kind* of eschatology that is associated with Jesus. The Kingdom is a direct reflection of the King. As Jesus entered the city of Jerusalem he had already begun the establishment of his Kingdom through such means as proclamation, teaching, and healing.

Everything that Jesus said and did was Kingdom centered. However, the popular understanding of messiahship and eschatology did not have sufficient space to imagine the *kind* of messiah that would die on a criminal's cross while bearing the sin of the world – much less envision a resurrection from the grave three days later. Just prior to his entrance into Jerusalem, Jesus took his disciples aside and spoke to them of his upcoming death and resurrection. Even though his words were plain and simple, the understanding of the disciples was closed and they had no clue as to what he was talking about.

When the Parable of the Minas is framed in terms of its eschatological message and function as Jesus completed his journey to Jerusalem, it takes on a fresh look. Jesus was only days away from a very cruel and painful death as a suffering servant kind of messiah. On the third day he will be raised triumphantly from the tomb as a newly crowned king kind of messiah. A mere forty days after that he would ascend to heaven and assume his reign – even against the ongoing opposition of those who do not wish him to be crowned king.

We find ourselves living in the meantime between the two advents of Jesus – one advent on each side of us. Living in the "in between time" is what this parable is all about. Understanding that the Kingdom is a present reality that is moving and flowing all around us compels us to give up control over our single minas so that they can be multiplied and replicated in a Kingdom that bountifully blesses. There is no blessing when we clutch our mina and wrap it in a cloth, bury it in the ground, or clinch it in our fists. Holding on to our mina brings its own form of judgment and death. In Kingdom life, we are not designed to grasp but to give.

Kingdom Now

The Parable of the Minas speaks to the shape of eschatology in our own times. The key to biblical eschatology is this – the future is a present reality. Much of our Christianized discourse has thrust eschatology entirely into the future without realizing that in doing so we miss the eschatology that is present here and now. We talk about eternal destinies as if they are totally yet to be experienced. These destinies are often thought to kick into effect the moment we die.

When our understanding of the Kingdom of God is whittled down to an event or experience that has not yet happened, we miss out on the reality that God is doing Kingdom work here and now. The point of the Christian life is to participate and partner with God in his present Kingdom work on the earth. Although it is often thought to be the case, the point of following Jesus is not so that we will not go to hell when we die. Rather, it is so that we can live in the Kingdom of God in our present experience and continue to live in the Kingdom when it is consummated in all of its fulness and glory.

Many of us who have lived within the clutches of the institutional church know our way around the institution more than we do the Kingdom. Some of the best tour guides of the institutional church have little capacity to offer guidance within the Kingdom of God. The religious leaders that were in constant contention with Jesus were more than adept at navigating religion, but they knew virtually nothing about navigating the kind of Kingdom life that Jesus had inaugurated. In fact, their Kingdom navigation system was so eschatologically skewed that they ended up leading the charge against the King which resulted in Calvary's horrific scene.

The Parable of the Minas speaks right to the heart of our misplaced emphasis of the Kingdom as a future only experience. The good news of the gospel is that through Jesus the Kingdom of God has already begun to appear. As followers of Jesus, we have already begun to live Kingdom lives. In the very same way, the powers of hell are already present in our world. Hell is not just the ultimate separation from God for those who are not "in Christ" – it is the separation of God that is experienced here and now.

We see this played out in the experiences of the servants in the parable. The servants who invested their minas in such ways as to have ten more minas or five more minas when the master returned understood that the master's reign as king had already begun. In light of this new reality, they invested their minas in such a way that reflected the presence of the kingdom. The servant who took no action whatsoever except to wrap his mina in a cloth and store it away, fully missed the point of the *kind* of king his master would be and the *kind* of kingdom that he would bring.

With the conclusion of this parable, Jesus' journey to Jerusalem was complete. What followed was nothing less than the very heart and soul of the message of the gospel that we proclaim and live. The crucifixion and resurrection of Jesus not only forms the center point of the story – it is the story.

What great news it is to share with a world that is lost in the chaos and darkness of selfishness, isolation, violence, desperation, and hopelessness, that there is a Kingdom of light, love, forgiveness, redemption, and reconciliation that is already here. There is no kingdom like it in all of human history and there shall never be a kingdom which shall be its equal. In this everlasting Kingdom of God, the powers of sin, death, and hell are forever defeated and the newness of abundant life and undiminished hope are without end.

During the "in between time" of the two advents of the King, the kingdoms of this world will continue to rumble and roll, but the days of all of them are measured and numbered. Living in the Kingdom of God does not mean that all of the other kingdoms are less real – only that they don't reign over the people of God.

As communities of faith forge ahead, the opportunity to align our language and our lifestyles with the Kingdom of God loom larger than ever. The reign of the institutional church has effectively been broken and we see God's Spirit working in new and fresh ways. With the weight of the institution being lifted from us and crumbling around us, we can become more open and more adept to being what we were when the whole movement of Jesus started at Pentecost – a living community of the living Lord in a world that God so deeply loves.

It just makes common Kingdom sense!

Step Inside

Parables have a way of putting us on a spinning wheel. When we step off, it may take us a few moments to get our orientation or to walk a straight line. Although we are standing on flat ground, the world inside of us is still spinning. In what ways did the Parable of the Minas spin your sense of justice or fairness?

This parable is about how we steward what God has given us in the "in between" times. Consider how the notion of living between the two advents of Jesus shapes your understanding and perspective on the world around you. In what new ways might your values or actions be challenged or shaped by the reality we are an "in between" people of God?

Popular understanding of eschatology is focused on the future events of what God is going to do. Biblical eschatology is focused on the Kingdom of God. This Kingdom was inaugurated with the first coming of Jesus. Although the Kingdom has not yet been fully consummated, we live in the reality of its very presence. What is a future reality that has already begun to arrive. In what ways does the reality that the Kingdom of God is already present among us impact your life and community of faith?

As followers of Jesus, consider how the Kingdom of God shows up in the world in which we live. In what ways do we see expressions of God's Kingdom among us? How we do invite our world to see and experience the reality of a present Kingdom of God?

Conclusion

The *way* of life in the Kingdom is very different than the *way* of life in any other realm. Jesus used parables as masterpieces of art to reorient our lives, our understanding, our relationships, and our commitments. These reorientations are fundamentally different than anything that is experienced apart from the Kingdom. However, the *way* of life in the Kingdom makes complete common sense when we become participants and partners in the Kingdom.

Although we might not have wanted it to be so, the long corridor of history reveals to us rather plainly that the institutional church is one of the places where the *way* of the Kingdom oftentimes finds fiercest resistance. This is not because people hate God or intend to do evil, but because the *way* of doing church and being good church members is often rooted in the kingdom of Christendom rather than the Kingdom of God. Christendom is simply the institutionalization over time of that which started as a vibrant and viral movement at Pentecost.

The parables of Jesus have always been held in high regard by the followers of Jesus. The twists and turns of these handcrafted stories get our attention not because they emerge from the world of fantasy but because they so powerfully speak to the world of reality. We cannot unplug from parables in the same way that we can from a science fiction movie. The very purpose of a parable is to issue an invitation to step inside. When we step inside, we do not experience a world of make believe fantasy but a world of grand reality.

Many readers of parables miss this simple point because most of us are wired to read the Bible with a literal, analytical, and logical mindset. Parables invite us to set those particular modes aside and simply enter the story of the parable. Our typical approaches to reading parables lead us to formal analysis and life principles that we can fit neatly into our Bible study lessons and sermons.

Regardless the amazing insights that we might garner as we read parables, the real point of it all is that we allow the parables to read us! The real interpreter is the parable itself. We are the ones being interpreted. The parables simply do exactly what they were intended to do – they expose both the reality of the Kingdom of God and the reality of the reader at the very same time.

When the reality of our own lives is revealed within the story of the parable, we cannot remain the same. Within the parable the highest realties of heaven meet the deepest realities of the human soul. In the unveiling of the Kingdom of God and the revealing of our own selves in light of the Kingdom, we are confronted and invited to a whole new world. It is a world that not only will be present one day as the Kingdom of God is consummated, it is a world that is already being realized and experienced in our current world.

Parables invite us to experience the living God within the context of the already present Kingdom as we live our daily lives. As we are transformed into Kingdom kinds of persons, we begin to see that the parables help us to make sense of the Kingdom. God's Kingdom is like none other and God's reign is benevolently supreme. The more we are a part of that world, the more that we begin to realize that the parables help us make sense of a world that is vastly different than the one that we have been so mightily shaped by.

Once we get a vision of the kind of God who reigns in the Kingdom and the kind of life that is cultivated in the Kingdom, it all makes sense! It makes sense that a loving God would call us to love even our enemies. It makes sense that a God of generosity would call us to live generously among others. It makes sense that a God who knows the deep pain of sacrifice would call us to take up the cross. It makes sense that a God who is totally committed to the mission of redemption and reconciliation compels us to live out that same mission.

As followers of Jesus and as communities of faith, we are called to be living parables of the presence of the Kingdom of God in our world. It is often challenging for those of us who have been nurtured and cultivated within the context of institutional church life to live as anything other than institutionalized church members. The reason that the institutional church has a knee jerk reaction against the Kingdom of God is the same reason that the Pharisees resisted the Kingdom. The Kingdom upsets and overturns our comfortable relationship with religion. It is no mistake that the Pharisees have appeared quite often throughout the parables whether as standing right outside the parable as part of the audience, or just inside the parable itself as one of the characters. It is likewise no wonder that the spirit of the Pharisees is alive and well within our sacred institutions of religion and still resists the impulse of Kingdom life.

Committing ourselves to be living Kingdom parables is perhaps the greatest gift we can give to our world. The world has seen enough of itself in the form of chaos, darkness, destruction, judgment, oppression, prejudice, violence, and even self-righteousness. As it always has, the Kingdom of God offers an alternative world that is rooted in love, goodness, beauty, justice, and reconciliation. These are the very things that we long for in our world but rarely experience. We are typically shocked when there is a moment of redemption in a neighborhood or on the world scene. We know that such moments are atypical and last only for a short season. However, these kinds of moments are the very norm in God's Kingdom and will last for all time.

What would our lives, churches, and world look like if we embraced the *parableness* of the Kingdom of God? Perhaps such lives would enable us to live beyond our church walls, worn programs, and religious pride. Perhaps we would avoid the temptation of reducing our faith down to doctrinal statements and church dogma. Perhaps we would see the Kingdom of God in faces and places we could have never imagined.

The yearning of our world is not for more religion in the midst of chaos, confusion, and clamor – it is the yearning for a Kingdom that offers the hope that humanity can somehow be reconciled and that creation can somehow be restored. These are the very things that the Kingdom of God both promises and delivers. Few things open the Kingdom of God up to us like the parables of Jesus. When we open the door and step into the world of parables, we begin to experience the Kingdom to which they bear witness. Once we have crossed the threshold, we can begin to experience the grand realities of the Kingdom. It is from within parables that we can see and hear that they are inviting us to a new reality where God reigns and all things are made new.

It just makes common Kingdom sense!

Resources

Barclay, William. *The Parables of Jesus.*

Bilkes, Gerald. *Glory Veiled and Unveiled: A Heart Searching Look at Christ's Parables.*

Blomberg, Craig. *Interpreting the Parables.*

Boice, James. *The Parables of Jesus.*

Culpepper, Alan. *The People of the Parables: Galilee in the Time of Jesus.*

Gowler, David. *What Are They Saying About Parables?*

Hultgren, Arland. *The Parables of Jesus: A Commentary.*

Kendall, R. T. *The Parables of Jesus: A Guide to Understanding the Stories of Jesus.*

Kistemaker, Simon. *The Parables: Understanding the Stories Jesus Told.*

Levine, Amy – Jill. *Short Stories by Jesus: The Enigmatic Parables of a Controversial Rabbi.*

Long, Thomas. *Proclaiming the Parables: Preaching and Teaching the Kingdom of God.*

Pentecost, Dwight. *Parables of Jesus: Lessons in Life from the Master Teacher.*

Price, Daniel and Erick Sorensen. *Scandalous Stories: A Sort of Commentary on Parables.*

Scott, Bernard. *Re-Imagine the World. An Introduction to the Parables of Jesus.*

Snodgrass, Klyne. *Stories With Intent: A Comprehensive Guide to the Parables of Jesus.*

Stein, Robert. *An Introduction to the Parables of Jesus.*

Webster, Douglas. *The Parables: Jesus's Friendly Subversive Speech.*

Wenham, David. *The Parables of Jesus.*

Young, Brad. *The Parables: Jewish Tradition and Christian Interpretation.*

Other Books by Brian Williams

Moneyball Church: Beyond Institutional Reign, 2022

Acts: Stories and Backstories, 2023

Brian can be reached at brian.williams@bgav.org

www.ingramcontent.com/pod-product-compliance
Lightning Source LLC
Chambersburg PA
CBHW060836050426
42453CB00008B/715